CHRIST

The Ideal of the Monk

CHRIST

The Ideal of the Monk

Spiritual Conferences on
the Monastic and Religious Life

COLUMBA MARMION, OSB

Voices from the Monastery

PARACLETE PRESS
BREWSTER, MASSACHUSETTS

2014 First Printing

Christ: The Ideal of the Monk

The Right Rev. D. Columba Marmion, OSB, *Christ, the Ideal of the Monk: Spiritual Conferences on the Monastic and Religious Life*, translated from the French by a nun of Tyburn Convent. Nihil Obstat and Imprimatur, February 11, 1926.

Copyright © 2014 by Paraclete Press, Inc. (this edition, which is abridged and features a translation slightly modified from the 8th edition of 1926)

ISBN 978-1-61261-573-8

Library of Congress Cataloging-in-Publication Data

Marmion, Columba, Abbot, 1858-1923.
  [Christ, idéal du moine. English]
  Christ, the ideal of the monk / Abbot Columba Marmion, OSB.
    pages cm
  "Voices from the monastery."
  "This edition, which is abridged and features a translation slightly modified from the 8th edition of 1926)."
  ISBN 978-1-61261-573-8 (trade pbk.)
  1. Monastic and religious life. 2. Benedict, Saint, Abbot of Monte Cassino. Regula.
3. Monasticism and religious orders. 4. Spiritual life—Catholic Church. I. Title.
  BX2435.M3813 2014
  248.8'942—dc23   2014024451

10 9 8 7 6 5 4 3 2 1

Published by Paraclete Press
Brewster, Massachusetts
www.paracletepress.com

Printed in the United States of America

CONTENTS

Preface

CHRIST JESUS IS THE SUBLIME IDEAL OF ALL holiness, the divine model presented by God himself for the imitation of his elect. Christian holiness consists in the complete and sincere acceptation of Christ by faith, and in the expansion of this faith by hope and charity. It implies the stable and total hold exercised by Christ upon our activity through the supernatural influence of the Holy Spirit. Christ Jesus, the Alpha and Omega of all our works, becomes by the communication of his own life, the very life of our souls: "living is Christ and dying is gain" (Phil. 1:21).

But besides the precepts laid down by Christ to his disciples as condition of salvation and essential holiness, there are found in the Gospels some counsels that Christ proposes to those who wish to make the ascension of the sublime heights of perfection: "If you wish to be perfect, go, sell your possessions, and give the money to the poor, and you will have treasure in heaven; then come, follow me" (Matt. 19:21). These are undoubltedly only counsels. "If you wish," said the master.

Still, the magnificent promises made by Christ to those who follow them show the value he attaches to their observance. Such observance has for its aim a more complete and more perfect imitation of the Savior. Once again, Christ is the way and the model, and spiritual perfection is the full acquisition and the entire taking possession of the soul by the teaching and example of the Word Incarnate.

These are the thoughts that I have endeavored to comment upon in the present volume. I have constantly placed the divine figure of Christ before the eyes of privileged souls called to walk in the path of the counsels: nothing is so efficacious as this contemplation to touch and draw souls and to obtain from them the necessary efforts in view of remaining faithful to so high a vocation and one so rich in eternal promises.

May these pages make a great number of souls better understand the nature of this perfection to which God so widely invites Christians, to increase in some of them the esteem of the religious vocation sometimes misunderstood by our age, to help some realize in themselves the call of grace, or to triumph over obstacles that natural affections or the spirit of the world oppose to its call. May these chapters, above all, animate the first fervor of such consecrated souls whose perseverance perhaps is wearied by the length of the way, obtain for those who are faithful to their vows the resolution of applying themselves without relaxing to attain the summit of the virtues, and stimulate the best of ambitions—ever unsatisfied—that of holiness!

CHRIST
The Ideal of the Monk

Chapter One

TO SEEK GOD

<hr>

WHEN WE EXAMINE THE RULE OF ST. BENEDICT, we see very clearly that he presents it only as an abridgement of Christianity, and a means of practicing the Christian life in its fullness and perfection. We find the great patriarch declaring from the first lines of the Prologue of his Rule that he only addresses those who wish to return to God under Christ's leadership. And in ending the monastic code he declares that he proposes the accomplishment of this rule to whomever, through the help of Christ, hastens to the heavenly country.

To his mind, the Rule is but a simple and safe guide for leading to God. In writing it, St. Benedict does not wish to institute anything beyond or beside the Christian life: he does not assign to his monks any special work as a particular end to be pursued. The end is, as he says, "to seek God." This is what he requires, before all, of those who come to knock at the door of the monastery to be received as monks. In this disposition he resumes all the others. It gives, as it were, the key to all his teaching, and determines the mode of life he wishes to see led by his sons. This is the end that he proposes and this is why we ought always to have this end before our eyes, to examine it frequently, and above all, only to act in view of it.

You know that every person, as a free and reasonable creature, acts from some deliberate motive. Let us imagine ourselves in a great city like London. At certain hours of the day the streets are thronged with people; it is like a moving army. It is the ebb and flow of a human sea. People are coming and going, elbowing their way, passing to and fro, and all this rapidly—for "time is money"—almost without exchanging any signs among themselves. Each one of these innumerable beings is independent of the others and has his own particular end in view. What are they seeking, these thousands and thousands of people who are hurrying in the city? Why are they in such a hurry? Some are in search of pleasure, others pursue honors, urged by the fever of ambition or the thirst for gold. The greater number are in quest of daily bread. Out of this immense crowd pursuing created things, only a very small number are working for God alone.

And yet the influence of the motive is predominant in the value of our actions. Consider two men who are embarking together for a far-off destination. Both leave country, friends, family, and landing on a foreign shore they penetrate into the interior of the country. Exposed to the same dangers, they cross the same rivers and the same mountains. The sacrifices they impose upon themselves are the same. But one is a merchant urged on by the greed of gold, while the other is an apostle seeking souls. This is why, although the human eye can scarcely discern the difference, an abyss that God alone can measure separates the lives of these two men. This abyss has been created by the motive. Give a cup of water to a beggar, a coin to a poor man, and if you do so in the name of Jesus Christ, that is to say from a supernatural motive of grace, because in this poor man you see Christ who said: "Just as you did it to one of the least of these who are members of my family, you did it to me" (Matt. 25:40), your action is pleasing to God. That cup of water, which is nothing, that small coin, will not remain without a reward.

Never forget this truth: a man is worth that which he seeks, that to which he is attached. Are you seeking God? Are you tending toward him with all the fervor of your soul? A person is worth what he seeks. This is why St. Benedict, who shows us the adepts of the cenobitical life as "the most strong race,"[1] requires so supernatural and perfect a motive from one who wishes to embrace this career: the motive and ambition of possessing God.

But, you may say, what is it to "seek God"? And by what means are we to find Him? For we need to seek in such a way that we may find.

To seek God constitutes the whole program; to find God and remain habitually united to him by the bonds of faith and love, in this lies all perfection.

Let us see what it is *to seek God*—let us consider the conditions of this seeking. For if we truly seek God, nothing will prevent us from finding him, and in him, we will possess all good.

We must seek God. But is God in some place where he must be sought? Isn't he everywhere?

As we know, God is in every being by his presence, by his power, and by his essence. In God the operation is not separated from the active virtue from which it is derived, and the power is identical with the essence. In every being, God operates by sustaining it in existence.[2] In this manner God is in every creature, for all exist and continue to exist only by an effect of the divine action that supposes God's intimate presence. But reasonable beings can know and love God, and thus possess him in themselves.

However, this kind of immanence was not sufficient for God as regards us. There is a more intimate and elevated degree of union. God is not content with being the object of a natural knowledge and love on our part, but he calls us to share his very life and his own beatitude.

By a movement of infinite love toward us, God wishes to be for our souls not only the sovereign master of all things, but a friend, a Father. It is his will that we should know him as he knows himself, the source of all truth and of all beauty. It is his will that we should possess him, the infinite good, here below in the dimness of faith, and above in the light of glory.

To this end, as you know, he raises our nature above itself by adorning it with sanctifying grace, infused virtues, and the gifts of the Spirit. God wills, by the communication of his infinite and eternal life, to be himself our perfect beatitude. He does not wish us to find our happiness apart from himself. He leaves to no creature the power of satisfying our heart: "I am your shield; your reward shall be very great" (Gen. 15:1). And our Lord confirmed his promise when, about to pay the price for it by the sacrifice of his precious blood: "Father, I desire that those also, whom you have given me, may be with me where I am, to see my glory, which you have given me because you loved me before the foundation of the world. . . . I made your name known to them, and I will make it known, so that the love with which you have loved me may be in them, and I in them" (John 17:24, 26). Such is the unique and supreme end to which we must tend. We have to seek God, not only the God of nature, but the God of revelation. For us Christians, "to seek God" is to tend toward him, not only as simple creatures who move toward the first principle and last end of their being, but supernaturally, as children who wish to remain united to their Father with all their strength of will urged by love, and through that mysterious participation in the very nature of God.

It is to this the psalmist alludes when he exhorts us to "Seek the LORD and his strength; seek his presence continually" (Ps. 105:4). That is to say, to seek the friendship of God, to seek his love, as when the bride looking upon the bridegroom seeks to see in his eyes the depth of his soul telling her of his tenderness. God is to us a Father of goodness. He wills that even here below we should find our happiness in him, in his ineffable perfections.

"To attain to God," this is the end that St. Benedict wishes us to have ever before our eyes. This principle, like a life-giving sap, circulates through all the articles of the monastic code.

We have not come to the monastery in order to devote ourselves to science, or the arts, or the work of education. It is true that the great patriarch wishes us at all times to serve God with the good things he has given us. He wishes the house of God to be wisely governed. St. Benedict does not wish the talents given by God to remain hidden. He permits the cultivation of the arts, a constant tradition that we ought to humbly respect, for the common good, for the service of the Church, for the salvation of souls, and for God's glory. But the end does not lie in this. All these works are only means in view of an end; the end is higher: it is in God, it is God sought for himself, as the Supreme Beatitude.

St. Benedict will have us seek God—seek him for his own glory, because we love him above all things. He would have us seek to unite ourselves to God by charity. There is not, for us, any other end, or any other perfection. The worship of God proceeds from the virtue of religion, doubtless the highest of the moral virtues, and it is united to the virtue of justice, but it is not a theological virtue. The infused theological virtues of faith, hope, and charity are the specific virtues of our state as children of God. Properly speaking, the supernatural life is based here below on these three virtues. They regard God directly inasmuch as he is the author of the supernatural order. Faith is like the root, hope the stalk, and charity at once the flower and the fruit of the supernatural life. It is this charity, whereby we are and remain truly united to God, that constitutes the end assigned by St. Benedict and the very essence of perfection.

This end establishes the true greatness of the monastic life; it also establishes the true reason of its existence. In the opinion of Pseudo-Dionysius the Areopagite, we are given the name of "monks," μονος, "alone, one" on account of this life of indivisible unity, whereby, withdrawing our mind from the distraction of manifold things, we hurry toward divine unity and toward the perfection of holy love.[3]

The ambition of possessing God—such is the primal disposition that St. Benedict requires of the postulant who presents himself at the door of the monastery. He sees in this a proof of a sure vocation. But this disposition must extend to the monk's whole life.

For the abbot, St. Benedict wishes that first and foremost he should seek "the kingdom of God" in charity as Christ commanded, that he should have care, above all to establish this kingdom in the souls entrusted to him. All material activity exerted in the monastery ought to have this one end in view: "that in all things God may be glorified,"[4] for in all things love refers everything to God's glory.

Let us carefully notice these words: "in all things," *in omnibus*. This is one of the conditions of our seeking God. In order for it to be "true," as St. Benedict requires, our seeking after God must be constant. We must seek his face forever. You may say: but do we not possess God from the time of our baptism, and as long as we are in possession of sanctifying grace? Undoubtedly. Then why seek God, if we possess him already?

"To seek God" is to remain united to him by faith. It is to attach ourselves to him as the object of our love. Now we know that this union of faith and love admits of a vast number of degrees. "God is everywhere present," says St. Ambrose, "but he is nearest to those who love him, he dwells far from those who neglect his service."[5] When we have found God, we can still seek him, that is to say we can always draw nearer to God, by an ever intenser faith, an ever more fervent love, an ever more faithful accomplishment of his will, and this is why we can and ought always to seek God, until the day when he will give himself to us in an inamissible manner in the glorious splendor of his indefectible light.

If we do not attain this end, we will remain useless and unprofitable. The psalmist says, and St. Benedict quotes these words in the Prologue in commenting upon them, "The LORD looks down from heaven on humankind to see if there are any who are wise, who seek after God. They have all gone astray" (Ps. 14:2–3). How many people don't understand that God is the source of all good and the supreme end of every creature? They have turned aside from the road that leads to the end. Why is this? What is a useless being? It is one that does not correspond to the end for which it was created. For instance, in order to fulfill the end for which it is purchased, a watch must show the time. It may well be of gold, studded with diamonds, encrusted with precious stones, but unless it keeps time it is useless.

We too become useless if we do not tend unceasingly to the end for which we came to the monastery. This end is to seek God, to refer all to him as to our supreme end, to place in him our sole beatitude. All the rest is vanity.

Let us seek him always, so as to be able unceasingly to put our lips to this source of beatitude. We can always drink from this source, without fear of seeing the waters exhausted, for, says St. Augustine, their abundance surpasses our need. Christ Jesus said they become in the soul "a spring of water gushing up to eternal life" (John 4:14).

Another condition of the sincerity of our seeking is that it be *exclusive*. Let us seek God solely. I look upon this condition as capital.

To seek God solely is the same as saying to seek God himself. Notice the term "God," not the gifts of God, although they help us to remain faithful. Not his consolations, although God wills that we taste the sweetness of his service.[6] We ought not to stop at these gifts nor be attached to these consolations. It is for God himself that we have come to the monastery. Our seeking will then only be "true," as St. Benedict wishes it to be, it will only be pleasing to God if we are attached to nothing apart from God.

There are many souls who have need of something with God, of something *more* than God; God is not all for them; they cannot like St. Francis of Assisi look at God and say with all the truth of their being, "My God and my all." They cannot repeat after St. Paul: "I regard everything as loss because of the surpassing value of knowing Christ Jesus my Lord. For his sake I have suffered the loss of all things, and I regard them as rubbish, in order that I may gain Christ" (Phil. 3:8).

Never forget this extremely important truth: as long as we experience the need of a creature, and are attached to it, we cannot say that we seek God solely, and God will not give himself entirely to us. If it is our will that our search be sincere, if we want to find God fully, we must detach ourselves from all that is not God and that would shackle in us the operation of his grace.

This is the doctrine of the saints. Listen to what St. Catherine of Siena said on her deathbed. Feeling her end approaching, she gathered her spiritual family around her and gave them her last instructions, which had been collected by her confessor, the Blessed Raymund of Capua: "Her first and fundamental teaching was that he who enters into the service of God, ought necessarily, if he truly wishes to possess God, to root out from his heart all sensible affection, not only for persons but moreover for any creature whatever, and tend towards his divine Creator in the simplicity of an undivided love. For the heart cannot be given entirely to God if it is not free from all other love, and if it does not open itself with a frankness exclusive of all reserve."[7]

St. Teresa, speaking from the same experience, says, "We are so miserly, so slow in giving ourselves to God that we never finish putting ourselves into the necessary dispositions. And yet our Lord will not allow us to enter into the enjoyment of so precious a treasure (the perfect possession of God) without paying a high price for it. There is nothing on earth with which it can be purchased." However, she adds, "if we did all that depended upon us not to cling to anything earthly, if our conversation and all our thoughts were in heaven, I am convinced that such a treasure would be granted to us."[8]

To find God, to please him alone, must always remain our fundamental disposition. It is only at this price that we shall find God. If, on the contrary, forgetting little by little our initial gift, we allow ourselves to turn aside from this supreme aim, if we cling to some person, some employment, responsibility, work, occupation, or some object, let's not be fooled: we will never possess God fully.

The nearer we approach God by faith, confidence, and love, the nearer we approach our perfection. As God is the principal author of our holiness, since it is supernatural to draw near to him, remaining united to him by charity constitutes the very condition of our perfection. The more we set ourselves free from all sin, from all imperfection, all creatures, all human springs of action, in order to think only of him, to seek only his good pleasure, the more too life will abound in us and God will fill us with himself.

There are souls who so sincerely seek God that they are wholly possessed by him, and no longer know how to live without him. "I declare to you," a holy Benedictine nun, the Blessed Bonomo, wrote to her father, "that it is not I that live, but another in me who has entire possession of me. He is my absolute master. O God! I know not how to drive Him from me!"[9]

When the soul is wholly given to God, God also gives himself to the soul. He takes particular care of her. One might at times say that for such a soul God forgets the rest of the universe. Let us, then, seek God always and in all. Let us seek him sincerely, from the depth of our hearts. Let us often say to him like the psalmist, "Your face, LORD, do I seek" (Ps. 27:8). And when created things present themselves to us, let us say inwardly, "Depart from me, for thou art the prey of Death."[10]

In finding God, we will come to possess joy.

We were made to be happy. The human heart has a capacity for the infinite and only God can fully satisfy us. "Thou did make us for Thyself, Lord, and our heart is restless until it finds its rest in Thee," wrote St. Augustine in his *Confessions*.[11] This is why when we seek anything apart from God or from his will, we don't find stable and perfect happiness.

In any large religious community, different categories of souls are met with. You will see some living in continual gladness. Their inward joy radiates outwardly. I am not now speaking of that sensible joy which often depends upon temperament, state of health, or of circumstances independent of the will, but of joy abiding in the depth of the soul that is like a foretaste of heavenly bliss. Have these souls never seen any trials? Have they no conflicts to sustain or contradictions to undergo? Certainly they have, for each disciple of Christ has to carry his cross, but the fervor of grace and divine unction make them endure these sufferings joyfully.

Other souls don't feel this gladness. Inwardly, and often even outwardly, they are troubled, distressed, unhappy. From where does this difference come?

Well, the first seek God in all things, and seeking him alone they find him everywhere, and with him, supreme good and unchanging bliss. The second are either attached to created things or seek themselves, by egotism, self-love, levity, and it is themselves too that they find—themselves, that is to say, nothingness, and this cannot content them, for the soul, created for God, thirsts after perfect good.

When the soul seeks God, and seeks him alone, when it tends toward him with all its energies, when it clings to no created thing, God fills it with joy, with that overflowing joy St. Benedict speaks about when he says that as faith, hope, and love increase in the soul of a monk, he runs "with heart enlarged and unspeakable sweetness of love, in the way of God's commandments." [12]

Let us then often repeat like that great monk St. Bernard: "From where have I come?" Why have I left the world? Why have I separated myself from all who were dear to me? Why have I renounced my liberty? Why have I made so many and such great sacrifices? Did I come to give myself up to intellectual labors? To gain knowledge? To occupy myself with the arts, or with teaching? No, we came, never let us forget, for one thing, and one thing only: to seek God. It was to win this one precious pearl of the possession of God that we renounced everything.

We should remain faithful to this sublime vocation. We will not arrive at the realization of our ideal in a day or in a year. We will not arrive at it without difficulty or without sufferings, for that purity of affection, that absolute detachment, full and constant, that God requires of us before giving himself entirely to us, is only gained by much generosity. If we have decided to give ourselves completely to God, without reservation, and never to bargain with him for the least corner of our heart, to admit no attachment, however slight it may be, God will reward our efforts by the perfect possession of himself. "With what mercy God treats a soul," says St. Teresa, "when he bestows upon her grace and courage to devote herself generously and with all her might to the pursuit of such a good! Let her only persevere, God refuses himself to none: little by little He will increase her courage, and finally she will gain the victory."[13]

I n this seeking after God, we cannot find a better model than Christ Jesus Himself.

But, you will quickly object, how is this? Can Christ be our model? How could he "seek God," since he was God himself?

It is true that Jesus is God, true God from true God, Light arising from Uncreated Light, Son of the Living God, equal to the Father. But he is likewise man. He is authentically one of us, through his human nature. And although this human nature is united in an indissoluble way to the divine person of the Word, although the holy soul of Jesus has ceaselessly enjoyed the delights of the Beatific Vision, although it has been drawn into the divine current that necessarily bears the Son toward the Father, it remains true to say that Christ's human activity, which was derived from his human faculties as from its immediate sources, was sovereignly free.

It is in the exercise of this free activity that we can find in Jesus that which we call "seeking after God." What are the innermost aspirations of his soul, those to which he refers all his mission, and in which he sums up his life?

The author of the book of Hebrews tells us. He raises for us a corner of the veil to enable us to penetrate into the holy of holies. He tells us that the first throb of the soul of Jesus on entering into this world was one of infinite intensity toward His Father: "When Christ came into the world, he said . . . 'See, God, I have come to do your will, O God'" (Heb. 10:5, 7). And we see Christ Jesus, like a giant, rejoice to run the way, in the pursuit of the glory of his Father. This is his primal disposition. Hear, in the Gospel, how he clearly tells us so. "I seek to do not my own will but the will of him who sent me" (John 5:30). To the Jews, he proves that he comes from God, that his doctrine is divine, because he seeks the glory of him that sent him. He seeks it to such a degree that he has no solicitude for his own. He has ever these words upon his lips: "My Father." His whole life is but the magnificent echo of this cry: Abba.

Nothing held him back in this search. At the age of twelve, he left his mother, the Blessed Virgin, at Jerusalem. Never did child love his mother as Jesus loved the Blessed Virgin. Put together all the love that can animate the heart of a son and it is only a flickering spark beside the furnace of the love of Jesus for his mother. Yet, as soon as it concerns his Father's will, or his glory, one would say that this love no longer counts for anything. Jesus knew into what an abyss of anguish he plunged his mother's heart during those three days, but the interests of his Father required it, and so he did not hesitate: "Did you not know that I must be in my Father's house" (Lk. 2:49)? These are the first words from the lips of Jesus gathered up by the Gospel. In them, Christ sums up all his person, condenses all his mission.

"R un," says St. Benedict, "while you have the light of life,"[14] carried along by the holy desire of reaching the kingdom where our heavenly Father awaits us. Press forward unceasingly in the practice of good deeds; that is the indispensable condition for attaining the goal.

In the same way as Christ Jesus, coming down from heaven, only finished his glorious course when he gained the height of heaven, we shouldn't grow weary as we follow after him in seeking God, in seeking him solely, until we arrive at what St. Benedict calls, at the close of his Rule, the "lofty summits of virtue" and "the heights of perfection." The soul thus "arrived" lives habitually united to God whom she seeks. She has a foretaste of the delights of ineffable union.

> O Lord, my God, my one hope,
>> hear me so that I may never weary of
>> seeking Thee, but that with unfailing
>> ardor my soul may ever seek
>> Thy Countenance.
> Grant the strength to seek Thee,
>> O Thou Who givest the grace to find Thee
>> after having more and more given the hope
>> of attaining Thee.[15]

Chapter Two

THE FOLLOWING
OF CHRIST

THE OBJECT OF OUR LIFE IS "TO SEEK GOD." THAT is our destiny, our vocation. This vocation is incomparably high, because every creature, even the angelic creature, is of its nature infinitely far removed from God. God is the fullness of Being and of all perfection and every creature, however perfect it may be, is only a being drawn out of nothing and possesses only a borrowed perfection.

Moreover, the end of a free creature is, in itself, proportioned to the nature of this creature. As every created being is finite, the beatitude to which it has a right by nature is necessarily limited. But God, in immense condescension, has willed to admit us to share his intimate life in the bosom of his Trinity, to enjoy his own divine beatitude. Placed infinitely beyond our nature, this beautitude constitutes our last end and the foundation of the supernatural order.

You know that from the time when he first formed man, God has called us universally to this beatitude. Adam, the head of the human race, was created in supernatural justice; his soul, filled with grace, illuminated with divine light was entirely set toward God. He possessed the gift of integrity by which his lower faculties were fully subjected to reason while reason was fully subjected to the divine will. All, in the head of our race, was perfectly in harmony.

Adam sinned, he separated himself from God, and drew all his descendants after him into his revolt and misery. All—the Blessed Virgin Mary excepted—are conceived with the imprint of his apostacy; in each one of us God beholds the trace of our first father's rebellion: that is why we arc born "children of wrath" (Eph. 2:3), sons of disobedience, turned away from God.

⁓

The consequence of this state of things is that seeking after God takes for us the character of a "returning" to God whom we have lost. Drawn into the original solidarity, we have all forsaken God by sin in order to turn to the creature. The parable of the Prodigal Son is but the picture of all the human race that has left the heavenly Father and must return to him. It is this character of a "return" deeply imprinted on the Christian life that St. Benedict teaches from the first lines of the Prologue to whomever comes to him: "Listen, my son . . . incline the ear of your heart . . . that you may return to him from whom you have departed." This is the well-determined and precise end.

Now, by what path are we to return to God? It is extremely important that we should know it. In fact if we do not take this path, we will not come to God, we will miss our end. For we must never forget that our holiness is a supernatural holiness, we cannot acquire it by our own efforts. If God had not raised us to the supernatural order, if he had not placed our beatitude in his intimate glory, we might have been able to seek him by the light of reason, and attain by natural means a natural perfection and beatitude. God did not will this. He has raised man to a supernatural state because he destined him for a beatitude that surpasses all the exigencies and powers of our nature. Outside this destiny there is nothing but error and damnation.

And what is true of the way of salvation, in general, is equally so of perfection and of holiness which are but a higher way of salvation: they likewise belong to the supernatural order. A person's

most finished perfection in the merely natural domain has of itself
no value for eternal life. There are not two states of perfection for us
nor two beatitudes, the one purely natural, the other supernatural,
between which we may choose. We must seek God as God wishes
us to seek him, otherwise we shall not find him.

This is one of the reasons why so many souls make such little progress in the spiritual life. They imagine holiness for themselves; they want to be the architects of their own perfection, built up according to their personal conceptions. They don't understand God's plan as it concerns them, or else they do not adapt themselves to it. These souls make some progress, certainly, because the goodness of God is infinite and his grace ever fruitful—but they do not fly in the way that leads to God. They go haltingly all their life. The more I come in contact with souls, the more assured I am that it is already a most precious grace to know this divine plan, to have recourse to it is a source of continual communication of divine grace, to adapt oneself to it is the very substance of sanctity.

Has God made known to us his will? Yes. As St. Paul says, he has revealed to us the "mystery hidden" (Eph. 3:9). And what is this mystery? What are these divine thoughts? St. Paul has disclosed to us the divine plan in four words: God has willed "to gather up all things in [Christ]" (Eph. 1:10), or better, according to the Greek term, "to recapitulate all things in Christ."

Let's contemplate for a few moments this plan of God for us and try to comprehend its height and depth, so that we "may be filled with all the fullness of God" (Eph. 3:19). God wishes to give us all things, to give himself entirely to us, but he only gives himself by Christ, in Christ, and with Christ. This is God's secret for us. Contemplate it with faith and reverence, for it infinitely surpasses all our conceptions. Contemplate it with love, for it is itself the fruit of love. It is because God loved us that he has given us his Son, and through him and in him, every good.

What then is Christ Jesus for us?

He is the way; he is the fountainhead of grace. He is the supreme high priest who has merited for us by his sacrifice the power to follow in the way that he has established. He is the fountain from whom we draw strength to persevere in the path that leads to the holy mountain.

We will first of all listen to the very words of the Holy Spirit. Next, we will take up in respectful parallelism the corresponding teaching repeated by the one who was, according to St. Gregory, his first biographer, "filled with the spirit of all the just."[16]

C hrist is the *Way*.

God wills that we should seek him as he is in himself, in a way conformable to our supernatural end. But, says St. Paul, God "dwells in unapproachable light" (1 Tim. 6:16). He dwells in very holiness. How are we to attain to him? Through Christ.

Christ Jesus is the Word incarnate, the Man-God. He becomes our Way (cf. John 14:6). This way is sure, infallible, it leads to eternal light, but above all, never let us forget, this way is unique, there is no other. As Jesus says: "No one comes to the Father except through me" (John 14:6), that is, to life everlasting, to God loved and possessed in himself in the intimate secret of his beatifying Trinity. So then, in order to find God, to attain the end of our search, we have only to follow Christ Jesus.

And how is Christ the way that leads us to God? By his teaching and example.

We must therefore know him. Jesus tells us: It is I who reveal my Father, your God; I know him, for I am his Son. "My teaching is not mine but his who sent me" (John 7:16). "I have not spoken on my own, but the Father who sent me has himself given me a commandment about what to say and what to speak. And I know that his commandment is eternal life. What I speak, therefore, I speak just as the Father has told me" (John 12:49–50).

The Father moreover confirms this testimony of the Son: "This is my Son, the Beloved; with him I am well pleased; listen to him" (Matt. 17:5)!

Let us then hear this word, this doctrine of Jesus. Let us say to him with ardent faith, we truly believe that you are the divine Word, come down on our earth in order to teach us. You are truly God, speaking to our souls. We believe in you, O Christ, we accept all that you tell us of the divine secrets, and because we accept your words, we give ourselves to you in order to live by your gospel. You said that if we would be perfect, we must leave all to follow you; we believe this and we have come. Lead us, Unapproachable Light, for in you we have the most invincible hope.

⟜⟶

A gain, Jesus is the way by his example.

He is perfect God, the sole-begotten Son of God, but he is also perfect man—he belongs authentically to our race. You know that from his two-fold nature flows a two-fold activit, a divine activity and a human activity, but these two are not confounded any more than the two natures are confounded, but they are ineffably united in one and the same Person.

Christ is the revelation of God adapted to our weakness. He is the manifestation of God under a human form. He is God living among us and showing us by this tangible human life how we ought to live in order to please our Father in heaven.

All that Jesus accomplished was perfect, not only because of the love with which he accomplished it, but in the manner he brought it to fruition. All that Jesus did, even his least actions, were the actions of a God and infinitely pleasing to his Father: they are consequently for us examples to be followed, models of perfection.

In imitating Christ Jesus, we are sure of being like him, although under a different title, pleasing to his Father. "The life of Christ," said a holy monk who spoke from experience, "is an excellent book for the learned and the ignorant, the perfect and the imperfect, who desire to please God. He who reads it carefully and frequently, attains high wisdom, and easily obtains . . . spiritual light, peace and quietness of conscience, and a firm confidence in God in sincere love."[17]

Let us then contemplate in the gospel the example of Jesus. If we remain united to Jesus by faith in his doctrine, by the imitation of his virtues, we will surely attain to God. It is true that there is an infinite distance between God and us; God is the Creator and we are creatures, the last rung on the ladder of intellectual creation: God is spirit, we are spirit and matter; God is unchanging, we are ever subject to change; but with Christ we can bridge this distance and establish ourselves in the immutable because, in Jesus, God and the creature meet in an ineffable and indissoluble union. In Christ we find God.

Jesus leads us to the Father. Never let us wander from this way, for that would be to run the risk of losing ourselves. But to follow it is to journey infallibly to the light of eternal life.

I t is not enough to know the way, we must also be able to follow it. St. Paul declares that the riches brought to us through the mediation of Christ, our redeemer, are inexhaustible (see Eph. 3:8). Under the apostle's pen, terms abound that express the manifold aspects of this mediation, and give us a glimpse of its inestimable treasures. Above all, St. Paul reminds us that Christ redeems us, reconciles us with the Father, and creates anew within us the power of bearing fruits of justice.

We were the slaves of the devil. Christ delivers us from this bondage. We were the enemies of God. Jesus reconciles us with the Father. We had lost our inheritance. The only begotten Son restores to us this inheritance. For a few moments contemplate these aspects of Jesus's work of mediation. These truths are doubtless familiar to us, but is it not always a joy for our souls to return to them?

But it did not suffice for our heavenly Father to give us his Son as mediator. He has appointed Jesus the universal distributor of every gift: "The Father loves the Son and has placed all things in his hands" (John 3:35). Christ communicates to us the grace that he has merited for us.

This divine life that Jesus possesses personally and in its plenitude he wills to communicate and lavish upon us: "I came that they may have life, and have it abundantly" (John 10:10). He wills that the life that is his through the hypostatic union should be ours by grace. Through the sacraments, through the action of his Spirit in us, he infuses grace into us as the principle of our life. Bear this truth in mind: there is no grace of which a soul can have need that is not found in

Jesus, the fount of every grace. We cannot work out our salvation without Christ, without the help of the grace that he gives to us. He is the one, the true life that saves from death: "the way, and the truth, and the life" (John 14:6).

These essential truths apply to salvation, but they are equally to be understood in the context of our perfection. You are perhaps surprised that I have spoken at such length of Christ Jesus before speaking of religious perfection. It is because Christ is the foundation of monastic perfection that he is the example of the perfect religious. More than that, he is the very source of perfection, and consummation of all holiness, "the pioneer and perfecter of our faith" (Heb. 12:2).

The religious life is not an institution created on the borders of Christianity. Plunging its roots into the gospel of Christ, it aims only at expressing the gospel in all its integrity. Our religious "holiness" is but the plenitude of our divine adoption in Jesus. It is the absolute tradition of the whole of ourselves through love, to the will of the Most High. His will is essentially that we should be his worthy children. He has predestined us "to be conformed to the image of his Son" (Rom. 8:29). All that God asks of us, all that Christ counsels us, has no other end than to give us the opportunity of showing that we are God's children and the brothers and sisters of Jesus. And when we attain this ideal in everything, not only in our thoughts and actions, but even in the motives from which we act, then we reach perfection.

Perfection can indeed be resumed in this inward disposition of the soul seeking to please the Heavenly Father by living habitually and totally in the spirit of its supernatural adoption.

⌒

Perfection has love for its habitual motive; it embraces the entire life, that is to say it makes one think, will, love, hate, act—not only according to the views of nature vitiated by original sin, but in the spirit of this divine "superaddition" infused by God, by grace which makes us his children and friends. The result of this disposition is to render all the actions of a soul, thus fully living according to the meaning of its supernatural adoption, pleasing to God, because they are all rooted in charity.

Listen to St. Paul: "Lead lives worthy of the Lord, fully pleasing to him, as you bear fruit in every good work and as you grow in the knowledge of God" (Col. 1:10). The apostle tells us we are to do this by walking worthy of the vocation in which we are called. And this vocation is to the supernatural life and the glorious beatitude that crowns it. (See 1 Thess. 2:12.) So, to please our heavenly Father, in order that he be glorified, that his kingdom be established within us and his will be done by us totally and steadfastly—this is perfection: "Stand mature and fully assured in everything that God wills" (Col. 4:12).

From where are we to draw the sap that makes all our actions fruitful in order that we may bring to the Father this abundant harvest of good works? This fruitful sap is grace, and comes to us through Jesus only. It is only by remaining united to him that we can be divinely fruitful: "Those who abide in me and I in them bear much fruit, because apart from me you can do nothing" (John 15:5). He is the vine, we are the branches.

You will perhaps ask how we are to "abide" in Jesus? By faith, first of all. St. Paul tells us that it is by our faith Christ dwells in our hearts. Next, by love: the love that, joined to grace, gives us up entirely to Christ's service and the keeping of his commandments. (See John 14:15.)

Perfection can only exist where the orientation of the soul toward God and his will is habitual and steadfast.

We find many obstacles to perfection in ourselves and all around us. This is why Christ Jesus said to the young man enamored of the ideal: "If you wish to be perfect, go, sell your possessions, and give the money to the poor, and you will have treasure in heaven; then come, follow me" (Matt. 19:21).

The religious, the monk, detaches himself from everything. He puts away all the obstacles that could halt his progress and shackle his flight toward God. Perfection has then grace for principle, love for its mainspring, and the degree of union with Jesus for its measure. Of this perfection Jesus is the initiator by the supernatural vocation. Second, he is its one model, at once divine and accessible. Finally and above all, it is he who gives it to us as a participation in his own perfection. We must be perfect as our heavenly Father is perfect, this is what Christ tells us, but it is God alone who can make us perfect and he does so by giving us his Son. Therefore all is summed up in constant union with Jesus, in ceaselessly contemplating him in order to imitate him, and in doing, at all times, for love, as he did. This is the secret of perfection.

St. Benedict lived on these fruitful truths. From these springs of living water he slaked the thirst of his great soul.

Go back to the beginning of his Prologue: he supposes that a postulant presents himself in order to be received as a monk and asks what he must do. St. Benedict replies that he must return to God by following Christ. "To you, therefore, my words are now addressed who . . . desires to fight for the Lord Christ, our true King." It is not a mere formula with St. Benedict; this idea impregnates the entire Rule and gives it its eminently Christian character. His Rule is Christocentric, so he tells us again and again "to prefer nothing to the love of Christ,"[18] "to hold nothing dearer than Christ,"[19] and, in ending his Rule, condenses all the ascetic program of the monk in a sentence of absolute devotion to Christ: "Let nothing whatever be preferred to Christ, Who deigns to bring us all alike to everlasting life."[20]

These are the great patriarch's last words, as it were, the supreme farewell that he bids his sons upon leaving them. These words echo those that open the Rule. Christ is the Alpha and Omega of all perfection.

So throughout our life, whatever be the state of our soul and the circumstances that may arise, we ought never to turn our gaze away from Christ. St. Benedict constantly places the divine model before our eyes. If he tells us we ought to deny ourselves, it is that we may follow Christ.[21] All our obedience—and what is the whole of our life but a continual obedience?—is to be inspired by the love of Christ.[22] Are we tempted? We must have recourse to Christ, it is against him as against a rock that we must dash our evil thoughts the instant they come into the heart.[23] Our tribulations, our adversities, must be united to Christ's sufferings.[24] The whole existence of a monk is to consist in walking in the path traced out by the divine master in the gospel.[25]

For St. Benedict Christ must be everything to the monk. In all things he would have the monk think of Christ and lean upon him. The monk is to see Christ in everyone, in the abbot,[26] in his brethren,[27] in the sick,[28] in the guests,[29] in strangers,[30] in the poor,[31] and, if need be, he is to pray for his enemies *in Christi amore*.[32] The love of Christ brought the postulant to the monastery and it is the love of Christ that keeps him there and transforms him into the likeness of his Elder Brother.

⟨⟩

May it be the same for us. May the love of Christ hold us united to him! There is no other way so traditional for us. Read the most authentic and most magnificent monuments of Benedictine asceticism and you will see they are overflowing with this teaching. It explains the ardent aspirations of St. Anselm toward the Word Incarnate, the tenderness of St. Bernard's love for Christ, the astonishing familiarities of St. Gertrude and St. Mechtilde with the divine Savior, the burning out pourings of Venerable Blosius to the sacred humanity of Jesus. These great souls so pure and high in holiness, made full demonstration of this line of conduct proposed by the great patriarch, faithful disciples such as they were: "To put the love of Christ before all things."[33]

This way of making everything converge to Christ, which is so characteristic of St. Benedict, is extremely advantageous for the soul. It makes the life of the soul powerful, for it concentrates it in unity, and in the spiritual life, as in everything, sterility is the daughter of dispersion. It renders it attractive, for nothing can more delight the mind and more easily obtain the necessary efforts from the heart than to view Christ Jesus.

"It requires very little experience of life to know how necessary it is for everyone to have ever ready some sort of idea or word or thought—which by practice comes instinctively to our aid in times of difficulty or mental stress and gives us courage and strength to walk in the right path. This—a veritable talisman to the soul if we will only let it be so—is to be found in the sacred name of our Blessed Lord. His should be an ever abiding presence to us, not a theoretical and abstract personality but a living actuality ever with us, 'Christ in the mind, Christ in the heart, Christ in the hands'—the abiding thought of Christ, the abiding love of Christ, the constant and conscious following of Christ—this secures the union of our souls with God and makes our service real and a work of love. . . . Of all the means which St. Benedict proposed to his disciples as aids to the spiritual life, this constant keeping of our Lord before the mind and following His example is perhaps insisted on most frequently and clearly."[34]

Chapter Three

COMPUNCTION
OF HEART

———

FROM THE FIRST LINES OF THE PROLOGUE OF THE RULE, St. Benedict, addressing himself to the soul, presents the monastic life as "a returning to God." You know the reason of this: it is that sin has, from our birth, turned us away from God says St. Paul (see Eph. 2:13). By sin, the soul turns away from God, the infinite and immutable good, to give itself to the creature, which is but transitory good. This is the definition that St. Thomas gives of sin.³⁵ If then we wish to seek God sincerely, we must sever all inordinate attachment to the creature in order to turn entirely to God. This is what St. Benedict calls "conversion."³⁶

Our holy father in speaking of "conversion" does not attach to the word the particular and precise meaning that we commonly give to it, but he views as a whole the actions whereby the soul, in turning away from sin and setting itself free from the creature and every human motive, exerts all its powers to remove the obstacles that hinder it from going to God and seeking him alone.

Between sin and God there is, as you know, absolute incompatibility. There is not, says St. Paul, any possible concord between Christ and Beliar, the father of sin (see 2 Cor. 6:15). And therefore to imagine that God will allow himself to be found by us, will give himself to us without our having to leave sin, is to be under an illusion. This illusion, more frequent than we think, is dangerous. We should ardently desire the divine Word to be united to us, but this desire should be effectual and urge us to destroy all that is opposed in us. There are some minds that find admirable—as indeed it is— what they call the "positive side" of the spiritual life: love, prayer, contemplation, union with God; but they forget that all this is only found with certainty in a soul purified from sin, from evil habits, and that constantly tends, by a life of generous vigilance, to abate the sources of sin and imperfection. The spiritual edifice is fragile when it is not based upon the constant flight from sin, for it is built upon sand.

Thus St. Benedict is careful to point out the necessity of working at personal self-conquest, the logical preliminary to all development, to all preservation of the divine life in the soul. And because in us these roots of sin, which are the triple concupiscence of the eyes, of the Flesh, and of the pride of life, are never entirely destroyed, this work never completely ceases; although in the measure that it advances, the soul, gaining spiritual liberty, moves more at ease, it still must never renounce vigilance.

〜

There are obstacles that prevent this union, so seeking after perfection requires that we first remove obstacles from our path. St. Benedict is explicit on this point: he puts within our hands the "instruments" destined to root out vices: "Not to give way to anger, not to harbor a desire of revenge, not to foster deception in one's heart, not to give marks of affection that are insincere, not to return evil for good, to keep one's mouth from evil and wicked words,"[37] etc. He likewise wishes that we should "daily confess to God in prayer, with tears and sighs, our past sins, and amend them for the time to come."[38] Then, he declares that it is only when the soul is purified from vice and sin, that the Holy Spirit will fully act within it, and perfect love reign as the principle of its life.[39]

This work of destroying sin and attachment to sin is necessary if we wish to go to God and find him alone. Let us then examine, with some detail, how we ought to devote ourselves to it. One of the best means of avoiding this perilous state is to cultivate compunction of heart.

For us, who are bound to seek perfection, this is of extreme importance. If so many souls make little progress in the love of God, if there are so many who easily acquiesce to venial sin and deliberate infidelities, it is because they are not touched with compunction. What then is compunction?

Compunction of heart is an abiding state of habitual contrition. Consider a good person who has given way to a grievous fault. Such a thing can unhappily befall us, for in the world of souls there are abysses of weakness as there are heights of holiness. But the Divine Mercy gives this person the grace of rising again. He confesses his sin with deep and true repentance. It is quite evident that at the moment when he grieves so sincerely at having committed this fault he will not go and commit it anew.

Look at the Prodigal Son on his return to his father's house. Do we picture him taking careless, free and easy airs, as if he had been always faithful. No, indeed. You may say: didn't his father forgive him? Certainly; he received his son with open arms without making any reproach. He did not say, "You are a miserable wretch." No, he pressed him to his heart. And his son's return has even given the father such joy that he prepares a great feast for the penitent. All is forgotten, all is forgiven.

The conduct of the prodigal's father is the image of the mercy of our heavenly Father. But as for the prodigal—now he is forgiven; what are his feelings and attitude? We can have no doubt but that they are the same that he had when, full of repentance, he threw himself down at his father's feet and confessed, "Father, I have sinned against you, I am not worthy to be called your son; treat me like the last of your servants." During the rejoicings with which his return was celebrated, those were his predominant dispositions. And if later the sense of contrition is less intense, it is never altogether lost, even after the boy has retaken forever his place in the paternal home. How many times he must have said to his father, "I know you have forgiven me everything, but I can never weary of repeating with gratitude how much I regret having offended you, how much I want to make up, by greater faithfulness, for the hours I have lost and for my forgetfulness of you."

Such should be the sentiment of a soul that has offended God, despised his perfections, and brought its share to the sufferings of Christ Jesus.

I t is almost impossible for a soul that practices habitual contrition to fall anew into a deliberate sin. The disposition essentially makes it repulse sin.

The spirit of compunction is precisely the sense of contrition reigning in an abiding manner in the soul. It constitutes the soul in the habitual state of hatred against sin. By the interior movements that it provokes, it is of sovereign efficacy in preserving the soul from temptation. Between the spirit of compunction and sin, there is irreducible incompatibility: compunction of heart renders the soul firm in its horror of evil and love of God. Thus St. Bernard more than once uses the term "compunction" instead of "perfection." So much does the sense of compunction, when it is real, keep one from offending God.

We cannot help being struck by the fact that the spirituality of past times communicated a singular character of stability to its adepts. While taking inevitable exceptions into account, it is indeed remarkable that the interior life of the monks of old, who were sometimes recruited from a much rougher class of society than ours, rapidly attained a great degree of stability, while with many souls today—even religious souls consecrated to God—the spiritual life is of appalling instability. The fluctuations to which it is subject are countless, and its inward ascensions are unceasingly meeting with opposition to such a point that all progress may be compromised.

The reason of this vacillation is most often due to the lack of compunction. There is no surer means of rendering the spiritual life firm and steadfast than to impregnate it with the spirit of compunction.

Yet it seems that, speaking generally, modern authors do not insist as much on this subject as did ancient ascetic writers who are never weary of dilating on the importance of compunction for spiritual progress. And we see the greatest saints constantly cultivating and recommending this disposition of soul.

Y ou yourselves know," said St. Paul to the Ephesians, "how I
lived among you the entire time from the first day that I set
foot in Asia, serving the Lord with all humility and with tears" (Acts
20:18–19). This was because he remembered how he once had per-
secuted the Church of God.

St. Paul does not fear to recall to his disciple Timothy how he
was a blasphemer and a persecutor. He declares himself the chief of
sinners. And, he adds, for this I obtained mercy. Remembering this
infinite mercy, he cries out in gratitude: "To the King of the ages,
immortal, invisible, the only God, be honor and glory forever and
ever. Amen" (1 Tim. 1:17)!

It was another convert, the object of similar mercy, St. Augustine,
who wrote: "To speak much when praying is to do a necessary thing
with superfluous words. To pray much is to knock for a long time
with the movements of the heart at the door of him to whom we
pray; prayer, in fact, consists more in sighs and tears than in grand
discourses and many words. God puts our tears in his sight, our sighs
are not ignored by him who created all things by his word, and has
no need of our human words."[40]

Our holy father St. Benedict echoes the words of St. Augustine.
"If anyone desire to pray in private, let him do so quietly, . . . with
tears and fervour of heart."[41] Again he says: "Let us remember that
not for our much speaking, but for our purity of heart and tears of
compunction shall we be heard."[42] Certainly our great patriarch does
not affirm this truth without deep conviction and I dare to say, an
experimental conviction. Look too at this portrait of a perfect monk

that he draws for us when he comes to the twelfth degree of humility: this monk, he says, has reached the point where the perfection of charity and divine union are about to be realized.[43] And what is this monk's attitude? He considers himself unworthy, on account of his sins, to appear before God.

This is truly what holy souls feel. A lady of high rank, who was converted after having lived in vanity and luxury, wrote to St. Gregory that she would give him no peace until he had assured her in the name of God that her sins were forgiven. The holy pontiff, full of the spirit of the Rule, answered her that her request was as difficult as it was detrimental: difficult, because he did not esteem himself worthy of having revelations; detrimental also for this soul, as it was in the interest of her salvation that she should not be assured of forgiveness [with an absolute certainty that excluded all doubt and cast away all fear] until the last moment of her life, when she would no longer be in a state to weep for her faults and to deplore them in God's sight. Until this last hour came, she ought ever to live in compunction and not to let a day pass without washing away her stains with her tears.[44]

See also our St. Gertrude, that lily of purity. She said to our Lord with the deepest self-abasement: "The greatest miracle in my eyes, Lord, is that the earth can bear such a worthless sinner as I am."[45] St. Teresa, formed to perfection by our Lord himself, had placed under her eyes in her oratory, in order to make it as it were the refrain of her prayer, this text of the psalmist: "Do not enter into judgment with your servant, for no one living is righteous before you" (Ps. 143:2). It is neither an exclamation of love, nor an act of sublime praise that we hear from this seraphic soul, who is declared by her historians never to have sinned mortally, but it is a cry of compunction.

With all these souls, it was not a question of isolated acts and transitory impulses. The words we have repeated were but the outward manifestation of an inward abiding sense of compunction eager to find outlet.

This habitual sense of compunction is so precious that, according to St. Teresa, souls that are the most blessed with divine favors are the most filled with it. Speaking of souls that have reached the sixth mansion of the interior castle, she puts them on their guard against forgetting their faults: "Souls to whom God has granted these graces will understand what I say," she writes. "Sorrow for sin increases in proportion to the divine grace received, and I believe will never leave us until we come to the land where nothing can grieve us any more. . . . A soul so advanced does not think of the punishment threatening its offenses, but of its great ingratitude towards him to whom it owes so much, and who so justly deserves that it should serve him. For the sublime mysteries revealed have taught it much about the greatness of God."[46]

Compunction inclines the soul to accept the divine will in its fullness, whatever be the form under which this will is manifested, and whatever be the trials to which it subjects the soul. The soul then regards these trials as means of avenging upon itself God's perfections and rights ignored or outraged by sin. It so much regrets having offended Love, that, if anything disappointing, hard, or painful befalls, the soul generously accepts it and this becomes an immense source of merits.

This sense of compunction is also the principle of ardent charity toward our neighbor. If you are severe in your judgments, exacting with others, if you easily bring up the faults of your brothers and sisters, compunction does not dwell in you. Indeed, one who is possessed by this sense sees only his own faults, his own weaknesses, just as he is before God. This is enough to make the spirit of self-exaltation die within him and to render him full of indulgence and compassion for others.

By awakening love, quickening generosity, and preserving charity, compunction purifies us and makes us more worthy of being united to our Lord. It strengthens our confidence in God's forgiveness and confirms our soul in peace. Thus it takes nothing away from spiritual joy and the amiability of virtue. Let us trust St. Francis of Sales who, better than any other, knew how to speak of divine love and the joy that flows from it. "The sadness of true penitence," he writes, "is not so much to be named sadness as displeasure, or the sense and detestation of evil, a sadness that is never troubled or vexed, a sadness that does not dull the spirit, but makes it active, ready and diligent, a sadness which does not weigh the heart down, but raises it by prayer and hope, and causes in it the movements of the fervor of devotion, a sadness that in the heaviest of its bitternesses ever produces the sweetness of an incomparable consolation." And quoting an old monk, a faithful echo of the asceticism of bygone ages, St. Francis de Sales adds: "The sadness, says Cassian, which works solid penitence, and that desirable repentance of which one never repents, is obedient, affable, humble, mild, sweet, patient . . . so that spreading over every pain of body and contrition of spirit, and being in a certain way joyous, courageous, and strengthened by the hope of doing better, it retains . . . all the Fruits of the Holy Spirit."[47]

These are the natural fruits of this compunction. Far from discouraging the soul, compunction instead makes it full of gladness in God's service. "God is quicker to hear our tears than the movement of our lips," says St. Augustine.[48] And St. Gregory writes, "God does not delay to accept our tears. He dries our tears that are but momentary with joys that abide."[49]

Penetrated with these same thoughts, St. Benedict wishes that we should each day confess to God, in prayer, with tears and sighs, our past sins.[50] St. Benedict does not say "from time to time" but "daily." Why does he make such a recommendation? Because he is assured—and he wants us to share this assurance—that it is on account of this humble attitude of a contrite soul that we shall be heard.

From wherever it comes—from the devil, the world, or our own evil tendencies—and whatever be its nature, we must, for our part, resist temptation with courage and above all with urgency.

Watchfulness has been sovereignly recommended to us by our Lord Himself: "Stay awake and pray that you may not come into the time of trial; the spirit indeed is willing, but the flesh is weak" (Matt. 26:41). Now, how are we to keep this vigilance? By the spirit of compunction, which keeps us ever on our guard. A soul, knowing its weakness by experience, has horror of anything that could expose it to offending God anew. On account of this loving fear, it is careful to avoid all that could turn it away from God who sees us night and day.

As it distrusts itself, it has recourse to Christ. He is a true disciple of Christ, says St. Benedict, who when tempted by the evil one casts him and his suggestions far from his heart, and brings him to nothing. And how are we to bring the evil one and his malice to nothing? By seizing the first "offspring" of the evil thought and breaking it against the feet of Christ.

Recourse to Christ Jesus is the most certain means of overcoming temptation. The devil fears Christ and trembles at the cross. Are we tempted against faith? Let us at once say: "All that Jesus has revealed to us he receives from his Father. Jesus is the only begotten Son who from the bosom of the Father has come to manifest to us the divine secrets that he alone can know. He is the truth. Yes, Lord Jesus, I believe in you, but increase my faith!"

If we are tempted against hope, let us look at Christ upon the cross. Is he not the holy high priest who has entered for us into heaven and intercedes with the Father on our behalf? He has said, "Anyone who comes to me I will never drive away" (John 6:37). When the devil whispers thoughts of pride, let us again look on Christ Jesus. He was God and humbled himself even to the ignominious death on Calvary. Can the disciple be above the Master? When wounded self-love suggests that we should return the injuries done to us, let us look again at Jesus, our model, during his passion: he did not turn away his face from them when they spat upon and struck him. If the world, the devil's accomplice, holds before our eyes the reflection of senseless, transitory joys, let's take refuge with Christ to whom Satan promised the kingdoms of the world and the glory of them if he would adore him: "Lord Jesus, it was for You that I left all things, that I might follow You more closely, You alone. Never allow me to be separated from You!"[51] There is no temptation but that can be brought to nothing by the remembrance of Christ.

If we thus act immediately, temptation will only have served to exercise our fidelity, to strengthen our love, and make us more pleasing to our Father in heaven.

But where are we to obtain this spirit of compunction?

To begin, by asking God. This "gift of tears" is so precious, so high a grace, that it is in imploring it "from the Father of lights" from whom every perfect gift comes down upon us, that we will obtain it.

The missal contains a formula *pro petitione lacrymarum*. The old monks often recited this prayer. Let us repeat it after them: "Almighty and most merciful God, who, to quench the thirst of your people, made a fountain of living water to spring out of the rock, draw from our stony hearts the tears of compunction, that effectually bewailing our sins, we may through your mercy deserve to obtain pardon for them."

We may also borrow from Holy Scripture certain prayers that the Church has made her own. For instance, David's prayer after his sin. You know how dear the great king was to the heart of God who had lavished his benefits upon him. Then David falls into a great sin; he gives to his people the scandal of murder and adultery. The Lord sends a prophet to him to excite him to repentance. And David, at once humbling himself and striking his breast, cries out: "I have sinned." The king then composed that inspired psalm, the *Miserere*, at once full of contrition and confidence:

Have mercy on me, O God, according to your steadfast love;
according to your abundant mercy blot out my transgressions.
Wash me thoroughly from my iniquity, and cleanse me from my
sin. For I know my transgressions, and my sin is ever before me.
Against you, you alone, have I sinned, and done what is evil in

your sight, so that you are justified in your sentence and blameless when you pass judgment. Indeed, I was born guilty, a sinner
when my mother conceived me. You desire truth in the inward
being; therefore teach me wisdom in my secret heart. Purge me
with hyssop, and I shall be clean; wash me, and I shall be whiter
than snow. Let me hear joy and gladness; let the bones that you
have crushed rejoice. Hide your face from my sins, and blot out
all my iniquities. Create in me a clean heart, O God, and put a
new and right spirit within me. (Ps. 51:1–10)

Such accents indeed cannot but touch God's heart. "But among all
those who weep, none are sooner consoled than those who weep for
their sins. In every other case, sorrow, far from being a remedy for
the evil, is another evil which increases it; sin is the only evil that
is cured by weeping, for it . . . the forgiveness of sins is the fruit of
these tears."[52]

To the prayer imploring the gift of compunction from God is naturally joined all spiritual means capable of awakening it within us: the most powerful is incontestably the frequent contemplation of our divine Savior's passion. If you contemplate with faith and devotion the sufferings of Jesus Christ you will have a revelation of God's love and justice. You will know, better than with any amount of reasoning, the malice of sin. This contemplation is like a sacramental causing the soul to share in that divine sadness which invaded the soul of Jesus in the Garden of Olives—Jesus, the very Son of God, in whom the Father, whose exigencies are infinite, was well pleased. And yet His heart was full of sorrow—"deeply grieved, even to death" (Matt. 26:38).

Let us often keep close in the footsteps of the suffering Christ, by making the "Way of the Cross." The gaze of Jesus upon the cross penetrates to the depths of our soul and touches it with repentance because we are made to understand that sin is the cause of all sufferings. Our heart then deplores having really contributed to the divine passion. When God thus touches a soul with his light, in prayer, he grants it one of the most precious graces that can be.

Chapter Four

SELF-RENUNCIATION

———

ACCORDING TO THE DIVINE PLAN THAT THE FATHER has traced out for us, he wills that we should only go to him by walking in the footsteps of his Son, Christ Jesus. Compunction of heart, as we have seen, by fostering the habitual detestation of sin, works efficaciously at dissolving the obstacles that would hinder us from following the divine model.

However, our inward dispositions must logically become a part of our conduct, ruling and inspiring our deeds. To sincere compunction will necessarily correspond acts of Christian renunciation. After all, didn't our Lord leave this teaching with all his disciples? "If any want to become my followers, let them deny themselves and take up their cross and follow me" (Matt. 16:24).

Let us then study the way that our Lord has gone before us, so that we, in turn, may walk in it. And if this way appears hard to our nature of flesh and blood, we might ask Jesus himself to uphold us. He is the Life as well as the Truth and the Way. By his almighty grace he will give us the power to contemplate him as we should, and to follow him wherever he goes.

Since Adam's fall, man can only return to God by atonement. In speaking of Christ, Hebrews says that he is "a high priest, holy, blameless, undefiled, separated from sinners, and exalted above the heavens" (Heb. 7:26). Jesus, our head, is infinitely far from all that is sin, and yet, he has to pass through the sufferings of the Cross before entering into his glory.

You know the episode of Emmaus related by St. Luke. On the day of the resurrection, two of Jesus's disciples set out to this town, a short distance from Jerusalem. They speak to one another of their disappointment caused by the death of the divine master, and the apparent downfall of all their hopes concerning the restoration of the kingdom of Israel. And behold, Jesus, under the guise of a stranger, joins them and asks them the subject of their discourse. The disciples tell him the cause of their sadness. Then the Savior, who has not yet revealed himself to them, says in a tone of reproach: "Oh, how foolish you are, and how slow of heart to believe all that the prophets have declared! Was it not necessary that the Messiah should suffer these things and then enter into his glory?" (Lk. 24:25–26)

Why then ought Christ to have suffered? If he had so willed, couldn't God have universally forgiven sin without requiring expiation? Sure he could. His absolute power knows no limits, but his justice has exacted atonement, and, first of all, Christ's atonement.

The Word Incarnate, in taking human nature, substituted himself for sinful man, powerless to redeem himself, and Christ became the victim for sin. This is what our Lord gave his disciples to understand in telling them that his sufferings were necessary. You know with what love and abandonment to the will of his Father Jesus accepted all that he had decreed. He suffered from his first entrance into the world so that he might fully accomplish this divine will. All was to be accomplished to the last detail with most loving faithfulness: "For truly I tell you, until heaven and earth pass away, not one letter, not one stroke of a letter, will pass from the law until all is accomplished" (Matt. 5:18).

But if our Savior suffered so that he might redeem us, it was also to give us the grace to unite our atonement to his own and thus render it meritorious. For, says St. Paul, "those who belong to Christ Jesus have crucified the flesh with its passions and desires" (Gal. 5:24). The atonement required by divine justice touches not only Christ Jesus; it extends to all the members of his mystical body. We share in the glory of our head only after having shared in his sufferings.

Having solidarity with Christ in suffering, we are to bear it for a quite different reason. He only had to atone for the sins of others. We, on the contrary, have to bear the weight of our own iniquities: "we indeed have been condemned justly, for we are getting what we deserve for our deeds" (Lk. 23:41). By sin, we have contracted a debt toward God's justice, and when the offense has been remitted, the debt still remains for us to pay.

T he spirit of self-renunciation assures perseverance. Every actual sin turns the soul in the direction of evil. Even after forgiveness, there remains a tendency, an inclination, latent for the moment, but real, which, engrafted upon our native concupiscence, finds the first opportunity of producing fruit. It is for mortification to uproot these vicious tendencies, to counteract these habits, to annihilate this attachment to sin. Mortification pursues sin inasmuch as sin is an obstacle between the soul and God. Therefore mortification must continue until these perverse tendencies are mastered. Otherwise, the tendencies will end by dominating, by being the source of numerous faults that will compromise, or, in any case, will keep at a very low level our union with God and the life of charity in us.

We have made a fervent Communion in the morning. Our soul is entirely united to God. But if, in the course of the day, in the midst of our occupations, the "old man" awakens to incline us to pride, to touchiness, to anger, we must immediately repress these movements. Otherwise we might be surprised into giving consent, and the life of charity, the union of our soul with God, would be lessened. Our Lord expects us to repress the ill-regulated movements that urge us to sin and imperfection. We cannot pretend to the state of union with God while also allowing bad habits to govern our hearts.

So, you see, renunciation is necessary, not only as a satisfaction for our past sins, but as a means to preserve us from falling into them again, thanks to the mortification of the natural tendencies that incline us to evil.

The need of mortification once recognized, we must learn in to what degree we ought to practice it—as well as how to appreciate specifically the value of the different acts of renunciation proposed to us. Their hierarchy is as follows: The mortifications that the Church prescribes; those that are prescribed by the Rule of St. Benedict, or are inherent to the daily observance of the monastic life; and then, those we choose for ourselves or that are sent to us by God.

First, the mortifications that the Church prescribes for us.

We find in a letter of St. Paul some words that at first sight seem astonishing: "I am now rejoicing in my sufferings for your sake, and in my flesh I am completing what is lacking in Christ's afflictions for the sake of his body, that is, the church" (Col. 1:24). What do these words mean? Is something then missing in the sufferings of Christ? Certainly not. In themselves they were, so to speak, measureless: in their intensity, for they rushed like a mighty torrent upon Christ. They were measureless above all in their value, a value that was, properly speaking, infinite, since they are the sufferings of a God. Moreover, Christ, having died for all, has become by His Passion the propitiation for the sins of the whole world (see 1 Jn. 2:2).

St. Augustine explains the meaning of this text as well. To understand the mystery of Christ, we must not separate him from his mystical body. Christ is not the "whole Christ," according to the expression of the great Doctor, unless he is taken as united to the Church. He is the head of the Church, which forms his mystical body. Hence, since Christ has brought his share of atonement, it remains for the mystical body to bring its share.[53]

Just as God decreed that, to satisfy justice and crown his work of love, Christ was to undergo a sum of sufferings, so he determined a share of sufferings for the Church to distribute among her members. Thereby each of them is to cooperate in the atonement of Jesus, whether in expiation of one's own faults, or in the atonement endured, after the example of Christ, for the faults of others. A soul that truly loves our Lord desires to give him this proof of love for his mystical body.

The Church naturally helps to legislate the work of expiation that concerns her as a whole. She has planned for all her children a share of mortification that notably comprises the observances of Lent, of Fridays, of the Ember Days, and Vigils. One who is less enlightened prefers his own mortifications to these, but it is beyond doubt that the expiations imposed by the Church are more pleasing to God and more salutary for our souls. This is because the value of our sufferings and self-denial is derived from their union, through faith and love, with the sufferings and merits of Jesus, without whom we can do nothing. Who is more united to Christ than the Church, his Bride? The mortifications she lays upon us are her own; it is as his Bride that she adopts and officially presents them to God. These mortifications become like the natural prolongation of Christ's expiations: presented by the Church herself, they are extremely acceptable to God who sees in them the closest and deepest participation that souls can have in the sufferings of his beloved Son.

These mortifications are also very salutary tor us. The Church herself tells us, at the beginning of Lent, that she has "instituted them as a salutary remedy not only for our souls but also for our bodies."[54] Don't forget also that in the course of the holy forty days, the Church prays daily for those who submit to these expiations. She unceasingly begs God that these works may be accepted by him, that he will make them beneficial to us, and that he will give us strength to perform them with the piety befitting disciples of Christ and with a devotion that nothing can trouble.[55] This constant prayer of the Church for us is powerful over the heart of God, and becomes a fount of heavenly benediction that makes our mortifications fruitful.

If then we wish "to be Christ's," as St. Paul says, let us accept, with great faith and generosity, these mortifications of the Church. In God's sight, they have a value and a power of expiation that other afflictive practices do not possess.

We shouldn't then be astonished that our great patriarch, St. Benedict, consecrates a long chapter of his Rule to the observance of Lent. He desires that during this holy season, besides the fast and abstinence, we should keep ourselves "in all purity of life; and repair the negligences of other times."[56] St. Benedict is careful to add to expiation that afflicts the body, inward mortification, and especially the exercise of that sense of compunction that is, as it were, the will to do uninterrupted penance.

After the penances instituted by the Church, second in importance are the mortifications and self-renunciation inherent to
the monastic state.

We must first examine the difficulties of the common life. However much it is sweetened by fraternal charity, however fervently
mutual love reigns, the common life still bears with it a great deal
of suffering. We love one another very much and yet, we jar on
one another. This is part of the very condition of our poor human
nature. Since sin entered the world, we are all, says St. Augustine,
men subject to death—infirm, weak-bearing earthen vessels that rub
against each other.[57]

Were there only in monasteries the holy, worthy of canonization,
they would still have to suffer from the common life, and this suffering can be much more acute in as far as the mind is more refined and
the soul more delicate. No community, however fervent it may be,
to whatever order it may belong, escapes this law, any more than the
greatest saints have escaped it.

Look at the apostles. Weren't they the best school of sanctity?
During three years, they were able to contemplate Jesus, to listen
to his teaching and be under the direct influence of his grace. Now,
what do we read in the Gospel? Two of them, to the exclusion of the
others, ask for a special place in Christ's kingdom.[58] Before the Last
Supper there is again "a dispute also arose among them as to which
one of them was to be regarded as the greatest" (Lk. 22:24), to such
a degree that our Lord has to rebuke them anew. Later, St. Peter and
St. Paul are at odds with each other. St. Barnabas who for quite a

long time had accompanied St. Paul one day as he preached to separate from him: they no longer agree. St. Jerome and St. Augustine do not always understand one another, anymore than St. Charles Borromeo and St. Philip of Neri.

Human nature has at times such weaknesses and deficiencies that even souls who sincerely seek God and are most united together in the charity of Christ are true subjects of mortification for one another. And this happens in every climate, in every latitude, in every community in the world. To endure this friction daily, with patience, with charity, without ever complaining, constitutes a very real mortification.

Our holy patriarch had great understanding of the human heart, and knew that everywhere human nature, even among the best of its kind, has its infirmities and miseries. So St. Benedict insists upon our duty of patiently enduring one anothers infirmities.[59] When these little dissensions arise, which he so accurately calls "thorns of scandal,"[60] he will not have us let the sun go down on our resentment lest it be given time to take root.[61] On this subject he introduces into the holy liturgy itself a practice inspired by the purest spirit of the Gospel. He prescribes that the abbot say the *Pater noster* aloud every day in choir at Lauds and Vespers, in the name of the monastic family,[62] so that when we ask our heavenly Father to forgive us our offenses, we may not forget in our turn to forgive our brethren if they offend us.

So true it is that the common life easily becomes a continual source of friction for our weak nature. But for those who seek God, this life is transformed into one of boundless and unremitting charity![63]

To the mortifications of common life are added those of the vows we make as a contract between ourselves and God.

Constant fidelity to our engagements constitutes a veritable mortification: we are, by nature, so inclined to independence, so fond of liberty and change! Faithful souls may observe their vows with gladness, fervor, and love, but this observance remains nonetheless an immolation for nature.

Look again at our Savior in his passion. He accepted it out of love for his Father, and this love was immense: "I do as the Father has commanded me, so that the world may know that I love the Father" (John 14:31). But didn't he suffer despite this love? Certainly. What suffering has ever equalled his? Hear the cry that escapes from his heart, crushed beneath the burden: "My Father, if it is possible, let this cup pass from me; yet not what I want but what you want" (Matt. 26:39). Love for his Father lifted him above the shrinking of his sensitive nature—and yet his agony was terrible, his sorrows indescribable. But because he remained fastened to the cross by love, he gave his Father infinite glory.

We, too, fastened ourselves to the cross on the day of our profession. We did so out of love, and if we remain faithful to our post of immolation, it is still through love. This does not prevent us from feeling pain. You may ask: isn't the monastery the entryway of heaven? Assuredly it is, but to stay a long time in a place of waiting, finding monotony and annoyances, can become singularly burdensome and require a big dose of endurance.

This is why we must remain firm and be patient till God's good time. God is never so near to us as when he places his Son's cross upon our shoulders, and we never give our Father in heaven more of the glory he receives from our patience than at these moments.

D ifficulties, disappointments, and contradictions will always be encountered in whatever part of the world we may be. It is no more possible to escape them than it is to abandon our human condition. St. Benedict, the most discreet of religious lawgivers, warns us of this. Although he wishes to establish in his Rule "nothing too harsh or rigorous,"[64] he does however ask the master of novices to show the postulants "the hard and rugged things"[65] that fallen nature will inevitably meet with upon the path that leads to God. But, he says,[66] like St. Paul, love makes us overcome in all things.[67] It is for your sake, O God, and to show you our love, that all day long we deny ourselves.

If we truly love Christ, we will not try to avoid the difficulties and sufferings that occur in the faithful practice of the vows and observances of our monastic life. We will embrace them as our divine Lord embraced his cross when it was offered to him. Some have a heavier cross than others. But however heavy it may be, love gives them the strength to bear it; the unction of divine grace makes them cling to it instead of seeking how to cast it away, and in the end they come to feel affection for it as a means of continually testifying to their love (see S. of S. 8:7). If a monk were to remain constantly faithful to what he first promised, if he were to live in a spirit of poverty and never admit into his heart a too human and too natural affection, if his whole life was spent in absolute dependence on his Rule and on those who represent Christ toward him, if he were to bear, without ever murmuring, the burden of the day and the uniformity inherent to the regular life of the cloister—this monk would give our Lord continual proofs of love and find God perfectly. But who will show us such a person!

St. Benedict exhorts us to offer to God, with the joy that emanates from the Holy Spirit, something beyond the measure appointed to us. Let us be happy to have the opportunity of offering God some acts of penance: fervor and joy should accompany what we give to God; magnanimity and generosity are joyful in the giving.[68]

However, before approaching the question itself of exceptional mortifications, we must understand the attitude St. Benedict recommends to us in general regarding the created things with which God surrounds us in our exile here below, and the legitimate pleasure we derive from them. The holy patriarch gives us a valuable counsel in this matter: "Not to embrace delights."[69] What harms the soul in this domain, is to give oneself up to them in excess. Christ partook of food, contemplated the beauties of nature, and enjoyed the charms of friendship, but he only gave himself to his Father and to souls. In the same way, self-renunciation forbids us to let ourselves be carried away in the use of created things. It is in following this line of conduct indicated by St. Benedict that we acquire, little by little, a holy liberty of soul and heart in regard to all creatures.

In the matter of voluntary mortifications, a certain discretion must be kept. The degree must be measured according to the past state of the soul, and the obstacles to be avoided. It is for a spiritual director to fix this degree.

It would be dangerous temerity to undertake extraordinary mortifications without being called to do so by God. In fact, to be able to give oneself to constant challenging of the body is a gift of God. And this gift often constitutes one of his most precious favors. When God grants it to a soul, it is because he wills to lead her far in spiritual ways. Often, he prepares her in this manner to receive ineffable communications of his grace; he delves deep down in the soul in order to empty her entirely of self, and possess her undividedly. Only, before entering into this way, it is necessary that we should be called to it by God. There is danger in entering it of our own accord. To be able to sustain great mortifications, we need a special grace that God will only give us if he calls us to it. Without this grace we break down physically and in consequence have to take special care of our health.[70] It is therefore with great wisdom that St. Benedict has prescribed that nothing should be done "without permission of the spiritual Father," for "every one has his proper gift from God."[71]

The domain where all latitude may be taken is that of interior mortification, which is also the most perfect. This mortification represses the vices of the mind, breaks our self-love and attachment to our own judgment; it refrains tendencies to pride, independence, vanity, touchiness, levity, curiosity, and subjects us to the common life, that penance of penances.

Consider the order of our day: To rise at the first sound of the bell; to go to the choir whether inclined to do so or not; there, to praise God with attention and fervor; then, to accept the thousand details of the Rule as they are laid down for work, meals, recreation, sleep. To submit ourselves continually to these things without ever murmuring or being in any way singular, forms an excellent penance that makes the soul greatly pleasing to God, and altogether docile to the action of the Holy Spirit. "He who desires for my sake to mortify his body with many penances," said the eternal Father to St. Catherine of Siena, "but without renouncing his own will is wrong in thinking that this is pleasing to me."[72] We only please God when we seek to do his good pleasure in all things.

Whatever be our mortifications, corporal or spiritual, those that afflict the body or those that repress the ill-regulated tendencies of the mind, they are only a means. In some institutes, exercises of penance and expiation play so preponderant a part that they constitute the very reason of their existence. These institutes have their own mission in the Church, for the diversity of functions, of which St. Paul speaks, exists for religious orders as it does for the individual. Those who make profession in these institutes are "victims"; the life of continual immolation gives them a particular character and splendour. Happy the souls whom God calls to the bareness of the cross! It becomes for them an inexhaustible fount of precious graces.

The spirit of St. Benedict is to form Christians who aim simply at practicing every virtue in a high degree without specializing in any of them. Our patriarch, in this respect, has quite other conceptions than some of those that prevailed with the fathers of the desert and the anchorets of the East in the matter of afflictive practices. Without neglecting, as we have just seen, exterior mortifications, St. Benedict's asceticism is brought to bear upon the virtues of humility and above all of obedience: it is to them that he chiefly looks for the destruction of the "old man" necessary to the fruition of the soul's union with God.[73]

Finally, one truth upon which it is important to insist here, in relation to exterior mortification, is that, although renunciation is an indispensable means, afflictive practices have no value in themselves in the plan of Christianity. Their value comes from their union through faith and love with the sufferings and expiation of Christ Jesus. Our Savior came upon earth to show us how we must live in order to be pleasing to his Father. He is the perfect model of all perfection.

Now the Gospel tells us he ate what was set before him, without making any distinction, so much so that the Pharisees thought it scandalous. And our Lord tells them, "it is not what goes into the mouth that defiles a person, but it is what comes out of the mouth that defiles" (Matt. 15:11). Let us then not place our perfection in exterior mortifications, even extraordinary ones, considered in themselves. What is above all important is that we mortify ourselves and bear our sufferings out of love for our Lord as a participation in his passion.

G od is the first author of our holiness, the source of our perfection, but we must labor at removing the obstacles that hinder his action in us. We must renounce sin, and the tendencies that give rise to it. We must free ourselves from created things in as far as they prevent us from going to God. One who will not submit himself to this law of mortification, who seeks his ease and comfort, who is anxious to escape suffering and does all he can to avoid the cross, who puts no constraint upon himself to keep all the observances of common life, will never arrive at intimate union with Christ Jesus.

This union is so precious that it must be bought with labor and toil and perpetual self-denial. We can only find God fully after having removed all obstacles from our path, and destroyed all that displeases him in ourselves. St. Gregory—whose words are evidently a commentary on the first lines of the Prologue of the Rule—says that in cleaving to ourselves and to creatures, we separate ourselves from God. In order to return to him, it is to Christ and to Christ crucified that we must cleave. We must carry the cross with him along the path of compunction, obedience, and self-forgetfulness. It is only by passing through the sorrows of calvary and the poverty of the cross that we shall come to the triumph of the resurrection and the glory of the ascension.[74]

As St. Benedict tells us, mortification and self-denial are but for a time, but the life that they safeguard and foster in us is everlasting. It is true that here below, where we five by faith, the splendor of this life is hidden from our eyes, but in the fight of heaven it will shine forever. There, there will be no more crying, no more suffering. God

himself will wipe away the tears from the eyes of his servants. He
will make his elect sit down at the heavenly feast.

Chapter Five

POVERTY

———

IN OUR SEEKING AFTER GOD, we are hindered by the obstacles we find on our way or within ourselves. To find God perfectly, we must first of all be freed from every creature in so far as it keeps us back on the path of perfection. The young man of the Gospel who comes to our Lord and asks what he must do to have life everlasting, is given this answer: "Keep the commandments." "I have kept all these," replies the young man. Then our Savior adds: "If you wish to be perfect, go, sell your possessions, and give the money to the poor, and you will have treasure in heaven; then come, follow me." At these words the young man goes away sorrowful. "For," says the Gospel, "he had many possessions" (Matt. 19:16–22) Riches held his heart captive and because of them he could not follow in the footsteps of Jesus.

Our Lord has given we monastics the immense grace of letting us hear his voice calling us to perfection. By an act of faith, we have come to him and have said like St. Peter: "Look, we have left everything and followed you. What then will we have?" (Matt. 19:27). We have relinquished material goods in order that, being voluntarily poor, we no longer have anything to hold us back. We may fully consecrate ourselves to the pursuit of the one, true, immutable Good.

God is so magnificent in his dealings with us that in return for the things we leave for him, he gives himself to us with incommensurable generosity. "Truly I tell you, there is no one who has left house or brothers or sisters or mother or father or children or fields, for my sake and for the sake of the good news, who will not receive a hundredfold now in this age—houses, brothers and sisters, mothers and children, and fields, with persecutions—and in the age to come eternal life" (Mk. 10:29–30). He puts no bounds to his divine communications, and this is the one source of our true beatitude: "Blessed are the poor in spirit, for theirs is the kingdom of heaven" (Matt. 5:3).

However, it is important that we always remain in that disposition of faith, hope, and love, whereby we left all to place our beatitude in God alone. It is important that we no longer be attached to what we have given up forever. And this is often very difficult.

As St. Teresa remarks, our nature is so subtle that it seeks to take back, in one way or another, what it has once given. "We resolve to become poor," she writes, "and it is a resolution of great merit, but we often take care not to be in want, not simply of what is necessary, but of what is superfluous, and to make for ourselves friends who may supply us. In this way we take more pains, and perhaps expose ourselves to greater danger, in order that we may want nothing, than we did formerly, when we had our own possessions in our own power."[75] You see, if voluntary poverty is an indispensable condition for finding God fully, for being perfect disciples of Christ, it is extremely important, in the course of our monastic life, not to take back from what we have given regarding the renunciation of exterior goods.

A nd yet has not man a natural right to possess? The simple Christian living in the world can fully use his faculty of having possessions without compromising his salvation and perfection— for, in this matter, it is not a precept but a simple counsel that our Lord gives when he speaks of leaving everything in order to be his perfect disciple. The action of divine grace in the soul of an ordinary Christian is hindered only by the ill-regulated attachment that makes his soul captive to exterior possessions.

But for us who for love of Christ, and in order to follow him more freely, have voluntarily renounced this right, it would be in some measure a sin to attempt to take it back unduly. We must have nothing of our own. Thank God for that, for it is a great grace to be fully detached. However, let us examine things more closely, for there is more than one way of having anything of one's own.

It cannot even be a question here of hoarding. At the last day we should fear to appear before God if we are in possession of something hoarded. But, without going so far as this, there are different ways of making any object whatsoever "one's own."

It may happen, for example, that a religious makes himself from the very first so difficult that he surrounds some book or other object with a hedge of thorns, so to speak, and in such a way that no one dare ask it from him. In theory, this object is for the common use; in fact, it has become the property of this religious. Little things, in themselves, but the detachment resulting from them can become dangerous for the soul's liberty. The principle of our perfection itself is at stake.

"Let all things be common to all," says St. Benedict. That is one of the characters of monastic poverty as he intends it to be.[76] By these words he refers to the community of goods that existed between the faithful of the early Church. He ordains that "anyone who treats the things of the monastery in a slovenly or negligent manner shall be punished."[77] Why this severity? Because the monastery being the "house of God," all things in it ought to be considered "as if they were the consecrated vessels of the altar."[78] Once more we see the deeply supernatural and "religious" character with which the holy legislator wishes to steep the monk's whole existence, even in the least details.

Let's return to that individual poverty which the monk ought to embrace so closely and let us try to enter more fully into its spirit. We understand it wrongly if we limit it to material privation. There are some rich people who are detached from their riches, according to the saying of St. Paul, "those who deal with the world as though they had no dealings with it" (1 Cor. 7:31). In the midst of their wealth, their heart is free; they are of those poor in spirit to whom Christ has promised his kingdom. There are some poor people, on the contrary, who covet riches, and cling with attachment to the little they possess; their poverty is only material. Have these poor people the virtue of their state? Certainly not!

As the kingdom of God is within the heart, it is above all in our heart that the virtue of poverty is perfected and developed: one can be poor while wearing the robes of a king. The man who is perfectly poor will be ready to seek God alone. Never let us forget that this is the end that St. Benedict points out to us: to seek God in the sincerity of our heart, that is to say, solely.[79]

T he practice of the virtue of poverty is inseparable from the virtue of hope. But what is hope? It is a supernatural habit that inclines the soul to regard God as its one good. "The LORD is my chosen portion and my cup" (Ps. 16:5). When in the soul there is living faith, it comprehends that God infinitely surpasses all earthly goods. As St. Gregory says, speaking of St. Benedict, "all creatures appear as small" to the soul that contemplates the Creator.[80]

Faith shows us in the perfect possession of God that precious pearl of which the gospel speaks. To gain it, we sell all, we leave all. It is a homage rendered to the divine goodness and beauty.

Faith blossoms into hope. The soul is so enamored of God that it no longer wishes for any other good, and the privation of any good, except God, does not trouble it. My God, you are my all and I need nothing besides you. I want nothing but you. I could not bear to have anything besides you for my heart to cling to. Like St. Paul, the soul counts all things as nothing. It also is not attached to the gifts of God, even though it may ask for them, not for their own sake, but because they help the soul to advance. Neither is it attached to consolations from on high, although God never severs it forever from the sweetness of his service.

The Christian who is poor and hopeful wants God alone.

Hope has another aspect: it inclines us to look to God for all that is necessary for our sanctification.

Monastic profession, as we have said, is a contract. When, having left all things for Christ, we remain faithful to our promise, Christ must, if I may thus express myself, bring us to perfection. He has bound himself to do this. God is a father, says our Lord himself. When a child asks his father for bread, will he give him a serpent? And "If," adds Jesus, "you then, who are evil, know how to give good gifts to your children, how much more will your Father in heaven give good things to those who ask him" (Matt. 7:9–11)!

And how true this is! If our heavenly Father loves us, what will he not give us? While we were his enemies, he reconciled us to himself by the death of his Son. He gave Christ to us that he might be our salvation. All that we can desire for the perfection and holiness of our souls we find in Christ Jesus. In him are all the treasures of the Godhead.[81] The indubitable will of the eternal Father is that his beloved Son should be *our* redemption, *our* justice, *our* sanctification. All his merits and satisfactions—and their value is infinite—should be ours.

Oh, if we know the gift of God! If we knew what inexhaustible riches we may possess in Christ Jesus, not only would we not go begging happiness from creatures, or seeking it from perishable goods, but we would deplete ourselves of them as much as possible in order to increase our soul's capacity for possessing true treasures. We would be watchful not to attach ourselves to the least thing that could keep us back from God.

L et us contemplate our Lord, who is our model in all things, whom we wish to follow for love's sake. What does his life teach us? He, so to speak, espoused poverty.

He was God, legions of angels are his ministers, and with a single word, he drew heaven and earth out of nothing. He decked them with riches and beauty, which are but a pale reflection of his infinite perfections. His power and magnificence are so extensive that, according to the psalmist's expression, he has but to open his hand in order to satisfy "the desire of every living thing" (Ps. 145:16). And yet this God becomes incarnate to bring us to himself. What way does he choose? Poverty.

When the Word came into this world, the king of heaven and earth willed, in his divine wisdom, to dispose the details of his birth, life, and death in such a manner that what most transpired was poverty, contempt for the things of this world. The poorest are born at least under a roof. He first sees the day as he lies upon straw. At Nazareth, he leads the obscure life of a poor artisan. Later, in his public life, he has nowhere to lay his head. At the hour of his death, he is stripped of his garments and fastened naked to the cross. His friends have forsaken him; of his apostles, he sees only St. John nearby. At least, his Blessed Mother remains. But then he gives her to his disciple (John 19:27). Isn't this absolute renunciation? Yet, he then finds a means of going beyond this extreme degree of destitution. There are still heavenly joys, but he renounces them, as his Father abandons him (Matt. 27:46). He remains alone, hanging between heaven and earth.

This is the example that has filled the world with monasteries, and peopled these monasteries with souls in love with poverty. When we contemplate Jesus poor in the manger, poor at Nazareth, poor upon the cross, holding out his hands to us and saying, "It is for you," we understand the follies of the lovers of poverty.

Let us then keep our eyes fixed on this divine poor one of Bethlehem, of Nazareth, and Golgotha. And if we feel some of the effects of poverty, let us accept this generously. Do not let us look upon it as a worldwide calamity! And let us not forget that we ought not to be poor merely out of convention, but because we have promised Christ really to leave everything to follow him. It is at this price that we will find in him all our riches, for if he has taken our miseries upon himself it is in order to enrich us with his perfections. Such is the wonderful exchange made between the Divine Word and ourselves. He brings his infinite riches, but he brings them to those who are poor.

We can never go too far in this voluntary detachment.

God puts no bounds to his graces: the kingdom of God is promised by Jesus to "the poor in spirit." This kingdom is first of all within us; it is established in us in the very measure that we strip ourselves of every creature and of self. All our spiritual life consists in the imitation of Christ. We need great abnegation in order to establish this disposition in us and never to seek the principle of our actions except in God—for our natural instinct urges us to make ourselves the center. But the life of our soul must be entirely subject to the divine good pleasure and must have no movement that does not come from the Holy Spirit.

This is what we ask of our Lord each morning at prime, on beginning the day. "O Lord our God, king of heaven and earth, grant this day to direct and sanctify, to rule and govern our hearts and our bodies, our feelings, our words, and our works, according to your law, and in the doing of your commandments. . . . O Savior of the world, who lives and reigns in the world, without end." We ask the Word to direct, to take in hand all that is in us, our thoughts, our feelings, our actions, all that we are, all that we have, all that we do. All that is ours will then come from God through Jesus Christ and his Spirit, and will return to God. We will bring our personality into subjection to Christ, in order to destroy what is bad in us, and to make all that is good converge toward the doing of his will. Then, without ceasing to remain ourselves, we will do everything under the impulsion, by the action of his grace and Spirit. It will be no longer in our self-love, our self-esteem, or our self-will that we seek the mainspring of our thoughts, words, and deeds, but in the love of Christ's will.

The same prayer contains the principle on which it rests, namely, that the Word is king of heaven and of earth. The Word lives and reigns in God. Christ lives where he reigns, and he lives in us in the degree that he governs all in us. He reigns over our faculties and rules our activity. When all within us comes from him, that is to say when we no longer think except as he thinks, when we no longer will except as he wills, when we act only according to his good pleasure, we place our whole selves in subjection at his feet. Then, Christ reigns in us, and all that is proper to us, all that is personal, disappears in order to give place to the thoughts and will of the divine Word. This domination of Christ within us must be complete. We ask this a hundred times a day: *Adveniat regnum tuum!* May that day come, O Lord, when you will reign entirely in me, and nothing within me will be opposed to the Holy Spirit's action!

Chapter Six

HUMILITY

W E ALL HAVE OBSTACLES WITHIN US THAT HINDER God's action. These obstacles are overcome by souls who renounce everything—created things, and themselves—who increase their capacity for what is divine by detachment from all that is not God. They look only to God for all they need. They are humble in themselves. They rely only upon God.

God fills them with good things. As to the others, they bear within them a tendency particularly qualified to form an obstacle to God, called pride. Pride is radically opposed to the divine communications. God cannot give himself to the self-satisfied. This is a fact we must face.

In studying this more deeply, we will acknowledge how necessary humility is for the life of the soul. We will understand how right our holy father, St. Benedict, was in wishing this virtue to be placed as the very basis of our monastic life. Then we will specify its nature and character. We will examine the "degrees of humility," such as St. Benedict defined them, and we will be enabled to follow the manifestations of the virtue in order to point out the means conducive to its development in our souls.

L et's ask Christ Jesus whom we want to imitate more closely, after
having left all things to follow him, to teach us this humility. It
is the virtue to which he especially wanted to draw the attention of
our souls.

One phrase of the Holy Gospel begins with these words: "Learn
from me" (Matt. 11:29). What is this that we are most especially
to learn from him? Is it that he is God, the sovereign being, all-
powerful, full of wisdom? Does he wish us to learn from him
the most heroic virtues, that he was obedient unto death, that
he delivered himself up completely to his Father's will, for the
interests of the Father's glory, and those of our salvation? Without
doubt he practiced all these virtues with wonderful perfection. But
what he wants us especially to learn from him is that he is "meek
and humble of heart," those virtues of self-effacement and silence,
virtues unperceived by human beings, or even disdained by them,
but which he urges us to make our own. Let us ask him that, through
his grace, he will make our hearts like his, for perfection lies in this
constant imitation, through love, of our divine model (Phil. 2:5).

Now what is it that the proud person does? He attempts to rob God of the glory which God alone merits in order to appropriate it to himself. The proud person lifts himself up above others, makes himself the center. He glories in his own person, in his perfection, his deeds; he sees in himself the principle of all that he has and all that he is. He considers that he owes nothing to anyone, not even to God. Sure, in theory, he may think that all comes from God, but in practice he acts and lives as if all came from himself.

This is the antagonism that pride sets up between man and God.

God cannot help but repulse such a one as an unjust aggressor. "For though the LORD is high, he regards the lowly; but the haughty he perceives from far away" (Ps. 138:6). Is there a more terrifying perspective for the soul than that?

Our Savior, so merciful, so compassionate, teaches us these same lessons again under the impressive parable of the Pharisee and the tax collector (Lk. 18:9–14). Look at the Pharisee: he is a man convinced of his own importance, full of and sure of himself. The ego of this man advertises itself by words and attitude. He stands in the careless posture of one conscious of his personal worth and perfection, one who owes nothing to anyone, and inversely, esteems himself to have need of nothing. He complacently displays before God all that he has done. Yes, he returns thanks to God, but, remarks St. Bernard, this false homage is only a lie added to pride: the Pharisee has a "tongue that makes great boasts" (Ps. 12:3), as the psalmist says. The contempt that he has for the Tax-collector shows that he believes himself to be more perfect, and it is to himself that he reserves the glory that in appearance he gives to God. He does not ask anything from God, because he does not consider he has need of anything.

Now look at the other actor in the scene, the tax collector. He stands at a distance, scarcely daring to lift up his eyes, for he feels how miserable he is. Does he think he has any plea that can prevail with God? He has none. He is aware only of his sins. He confides only in the divine mercy. He looks for nothing; all his confidence, all his hope, is placed in God.

Now, how does God act with these two men? Quite differently. "I tell you," Christ declare, "this man [the tax collector] went down to his home justified rather than the other" (Lk. 18:14). Was not the tax collector, however, a sinner? Assuredly. The Pharisee, on the other hand, was he not, at least outwardly, a faithful observer of the Law of Moses? No less certainly he was. But the Pharisee, full of himself, showed by his contempt of the tax collector that he was puffed up in his own heart by reason of the good works he had done. Therefore God repulses him. To the poor tax collector who humbles himself, on the contrary, Jesus gives an abundance of grace.

Jesus, in ending the parable of the Pharisee and the tax collector, lays down the fundamental law that rules our relations with God. He brings forward the essential lesson we have to learn: "All who exalt themselves will be humbled, but all who humble themselves will be exalted" (Lk. 18:14).

It is pride that above all prevents God from giving himself. If there were no longer any pride in souls, God would give himself to them fully. Humility is so fundamental a virtue that without it, says St. Bernard of Clairvaux, all other virtues go to ruin.[82] This is because, by reason of our fallen nature, there are obstacles in us opposed to the expansion of the inner life. If these obstacles are not removed, they end by stifling the virtues. The greatest obstacle is pride, because it is a fundamentally and radically opposed to divine union itself. For that reason, humility, again says St. Bernard, receives the other virtues, guards and perfects them.[83]

The humble soul is ready to receive all the gifts of God because it is empty of self and looks to God for all that is necessary for its perfection. It is also ready because it feels itself to be poor and miserable. God, beholding our fallenness, encompassed with weaknesses, subject to temptation, is touched by this misery, as if it were his own. This divine movement that inclines the Lord toward our misery in order to relieve it is mercy.

Each one of us has a sum of miseries sufficient to draw down the pity of our God. We are like that poor wayfarer lying on the road to Jericho, stripped of his garments, covered with wounds. By original sin, we have all been stripped of grace; our personal sins have covered our soul with wounds, but Christ has been for us the Good Samaritan. He came to heal us, to pour the balm of his precious blood upon our wounds, to take us into his arms and entrust us to the tenderness of his Church.

When we acknowledge that we are weak and poor, we implicitly proclaim God's power, wisdom, and holiness. It is rendering homage to the divine plenitude, and this homage is so pleasing to God that he stoops toward the humble soul to fill it with good things. As St. Bernard says, "Our heart is a vessel, destined to receive grace. In order for it to contain grace in abundance it must be empty of self-love and vainglory."[84]

There exists another reason for God's liberality toward humble souls. God sees that the humble soul will not, as the proud does, appropriate to itself the divine gifts, but will return all glory and praise to heaven. This is why God has no hesitation in causing the abundance of his favors to flow into a humble soul; it will not abuse them; it will not use them other than as God intends.

The nearer we want to draw to God, the more deeply we must anchor ourselves in humility. St. Augustine shows us this very clearly in a familiar comparison. "The end," he says, "that we pursue is very great; for it is God whom we seek, to whom we would attain, for in him alone is to be found our eternal beatitude. We can only come to this lofty end through humility. Do you wish to raise yourself? Begin by humbling yourself."[85]

By this, we can easily understand St. Benedict, who assigns to us no other end than "to find God," founding our spiritual life upon humility. He had himself reached too near God to be ignorant that humility alone draws down grace, and that without grace we can do nothing. All the asceticism of St. Benedict consists in making the soul humble, then in making it live in obedience (which is the practical expression of humility). This will be for it the secret of intimate union with God.[86]

St. Benedict devotes a whole chapter to this fundamental virtue, but he has a sure and wide concept of humility. He does not envisage it simply as a virtue apart, linked to the moral virtue of temperance,[87] but as a virtue expressing the whole attitude the soul ought to have in face of God, an attitude that should animate us as creatures and as adopted children, an attitude on which all our spiritual life is to be based.

The theory of humility is, with St. Benedict, exactly correlative with his conception of grace. The progress of the soul in God is the progress of God in the soul. The work, which by means of grace, belongs properly speaking to the soul is to open the way to God's action, to open itself to God. To every degree of ascension toward God corresponds a degree of "the opening of self to God." How do we open ourselves to God? By more and more abolishing pride within us, by more and more deepening humility. And this is how, definitively, the ladder of humility, in the negative sense, can serve as the ladder, in the positive sense, of perfection and charity.

St. Benedict compares a proud person repulsed by God to an infant weaned too soon from its mother. Severed from the source of life, the infant is doomed to perish. This is the great danger that the soul risks: to be separated from God, the sole fount of every grace. If then, continues our Holy Father, "we wish to attain to the summit of supreme humility, and speedily reach that heavenly exaltation to which we ascend by the humility of this present life, we must by ever ascending degrees of action, erect the ladder that appeared to Jacob while he slept and by which he saw the angels descending and ascending."[88] Next, St. Benedict compares the two sides of the ladder to the body and the soul, for the body is to share in the inward virtue, and divine grace has placed between these two sides the various degrees that we must climb.

Before studying these degrees with St. Benedict, let us first say what humility is. St. Benedict does not define it. Instead, he points out its different manifestations. We will therefore borrow the elements of the definition of humility from St. Thomas, who in his *Summa theologica* comments on this chapter of St. Benedict and justifies the degrees of humility indicated by him.[89] God sometimes gives to a soul, all at once, a higher degree of humility, as he gives to another the gift of prayer, St. Thomas says. But in the ordinary way, God requires our cooperation. And since we only esteem and seek what we know, let us try to understand clearly what this virtue is.

Humility can thus be defined as a moral virtue that inclines us, from reverence toward God, to abase ourselves and keep ourselves in the place that we see is due. Very logically, then, St. Benedict tells us that if "we see any good in ourselves we ought to attribute it to God and not to ourselves." And, he adds, we ought on the contrary to impute to ourselves all the evil that we do and of which we know we are the cause.[90] Indeed, what is never from God and is exclusively ours is sin.

Such is the condition that the infallible light of faith shows us as being our own when we consider all things from the point of view of divine truth. Humility keeps us in an attitude conformable with this condition. The will, aided by grace, prompts us to keep in the place which is properly "our own."

St. Thomas says that the principal reason and motive of this self-abasement is "reverence towards God."[91] We here touch on the deepest point, the very root of the virtue.

When in prayer we contemplate the perfections and works of God, when a ray of divine light reaches us, what is the first movement of the soul touched by grace? It is one of self-abasement; the soul is lost in adoration. This attitude of adoration is the only "true" one that the creature, as such, can have before God.

What is adoration? It is the avowal of our inferiority before the Divine. It is the acknowledgment of our absolute dependence in face of him who alone is the plenitude of being. It is the homage of our subjection in face of the infinite sovereignty. When a creature does not remain in this attitude, it is not in the truth.

The soul understands, under a strong inner light, what a close contact there may be between itself and God. It beholds the infinite contrast of the two: littleness and lowliness contrasted with greatness and majesty, greatness and majesty contrasted with littleness and lowliness. The soul may concentrate its attention the more upon the one or other of these two terms of the relation. If it is upon God, then it tends to adore him. It is at the precise instant of our self-annihilation in presence of the Divine that humility is born in the soul. As soon as reverence toward God fills the soul, humility springs.[92]

⌐⌐⌐⌐⌐⌐

T he fear of God is said to constitute the first of all the degrees of
humility: because without it humility cannot be born or maintained. St. Benedict places reverence toward God as the point of
departure: "The first degree of humility consists in having the fear of
God ever before our eyes, without ever forgetting it."[93] But there is a
gradation in the fear of God. It cannot be a question of only servile
fear, of the fear of chastisement, proper to the slave, excluding love
and paralyzing confidence.

The fear of God concerns, first of all, reverence. This fear makes
us watch unceasingly to avoid sin, in order not to displease God who
punishes evil. This fear is good. Scripture places this prayer upon
our lips: "My flesh trembles for fear of you, and I am afraid of your
judgments" (Ps. 119:120).

Undoubtedly, as the soul progresses in the spiritual life, the previous fear gives way, little by little, to love, as the habitual mainspring
of action. It never ought, however, to disappear altogether; it is a
weapon that we should constantly hold in reserve, in our spiritual
arsenal, for hours of combat when love threatens to be overcome by
passion. The Council of Trent insists upon the uncertainty in which
we are left touching our final perseverance. Our life is a continual
trial of faith, and we ought never to part with, or fail to keep within
our reach, the weapon of the fear of God.

This imperfect fear ought however to culminate habitually in the
reverential fear in which the ultimate term is adoration full of love.
It is of this fear that is said: "The fear of the LORD is the beginning
of wisdom; all those who practice it have a good understanding"

(Ps. 111:10). It is the reverence that seizes every creature before the infinite plenitude of the Divine, even when this creature has become a child of God, even when admitted to the kingdom of heaven. This is a reverence that makes the purest angels veil their faces before the dazzling effulgence of the Divine, a reverence that filled the very humanity of Christ.

What does St. Benedict say to us when he invites us in the Prologue to place ourselves in his school? He wishes to teach us, as his sons, the fear of God.[94] God is a Father full of goodness, to whose admonitions we ought to listen with the ears of the heart, that is to say, with a lively sense of love, for this Father prepares for us an inheritance of immortal glory and eternal beatitude. St. Benedict would have us take care not to weary with our faults, for the goodness of this heavenly Father awaits us, and in his love, destines those who fear him to an ineffable participation in his own life.

This fear, this reverence toward God, the Father of infinite majesty, ought to be habitual and constant, for it concerns the virtue, that is to say, a habitual disposition, and not an isolated act.

⌣⟶

B ut it is necessary for us to be sincere with ourselves before God. We ought to watch over the movements of our soul lest any falsehood in our attitude or dealings escape us. We should be true in the sanctuary of ourselves in face of God. This is a great duty. We should never tolerate the least insincerity within ourselves.

We are so small a thing before God. We are incapable of doing anything without the grace of Christ Jesus. It alone gives worth to our deeds. If, practically, we believe that we do a great deal by ourselves, that we have a right to consideration because we have rendered such or such service, we have yet not arrived at humility. St. Benedict does not hesitate to deal rigorously, on occasion, with these persistent forms of the spirit of self-exaltation. If, he says, among those who exercise an art or craft in the monastery, there be any who are tempted to pride about their attainments and skill, or on the benefit that the monastery derives from them, they will be forever forbidden to work at this art or craft, rather than expose their souls to spiritual harm.

A monk should believe himself, sincerely and from the bottom of his heart, to be the last of all men. This is St. Paul's counsel: "In humility regard others as better than yourselves" (Phil. 2:3).

Few souls arrive at this height and live there habitually; it is assuredly a gift of God. And it is necessary, so that the light of the Holy Spirit may give the soul an intensely clear view of the divine perfections. Seeing the nothingness that it truly is in presence of the Divine, and considering the gifts of God in others, the soul inwardly places itself at the feet of all. Whoever mounts toward this degree will keep himself, in every circumstance, from judging himself better than others and from being severe toward them. If God had acted with rigor toward us, if he had treated us according to strict justice, what would have become of us? Why are we so sure of ourselves? We must also consider the possibilities of evil that are to be found in us. May not one whom we are tempted to despise today soon become better than we are? Also, can we be sure of what our dispositions will be tomorrow? Within us all, poor creatures that we are, there is a constant principle of instability and deficiency that we have unceasingly to combat with the help of grace and the exercise of humility.

Now I must approach an important point: humility is truth. As St. Teresa of Avila says, "Some think it humility not to believe that God is bestowing his gifts upon them." Is this honoring God? Not a chance.

"Let us clearly understand," adds the saint, "that it is perfectly clear God bestows his gifts without any merit whatever on our part." What are we then to do in presence of divine graces? Recognize that God alone is the author and principle of them and thank him with grateful hearts. "For if we do not recognize the gifts received at his hands, we will never be moved to love him. It is a most certain truth that the richer we see ourselves to be, confessing at the same time our poverty, the greater will be our progress, and the more real our humility . . . if we walk in simplicity before God, aiming at pleasing him only, and not men."[95]

Even more important, true humility does not deceive itself. It does not deny God's gifts. It uses them, but returns all glory to him from whom they come. Look at the Blessed Virgin Mary, chosen from among all women to be the mother of the Word Incarnate. No creature, after the humanity of Jesus, has been filled with graces as she was. She was surely conscious of this. So, when Elizabeth congratulates her on her divine maternity, does the Blessed Virgin deny the signal favor of which she is the object? Indeed not. She even acknowledges that it is a unique privilege, that "the Mighty One has done great things for me" (Lk. 1:49), things so great, so marvelous that all generations will call her blessed. But, just as she does not deny these graces, neither does she make them an occasion of glorifying herself. She returns all the glory to God, who works them in her. This is the way the humble soul acts.

⟨⟩

S t. Benedict's teaching is inspired with exactly the same spirit. "Let the good that one sees in oneself," he says, "be attributed to God and not to oneself."[96] He does not deny that we may be aware of the divine gifts within us; far from binding us to veil them from ourselves, he allows them to be seen. And having seen them we will feel urged to use them on every occasion in the service of he who has distributed them to us. But we must not imagine they are due to us, but thank God for them.

The holy patriarch is still more explicit in his Prologue: those who seek God, he says, fear the Lord (that is, the root of humility); they do not pride themselves on their good observance. Knowing that the good in them does not come from themselves but from the Lord, they glorify him for what he divinely works in them, saying with the psalmist: "Not to us, O LORD, not to us, but to your name give glory, for the sake of your steadfast love and your faithfulness" (Ps. 115:1).

"It is contrary to humility," St. Thomas adds, "for a person to tend to things too high for him, relying on his own strength. But if he puts his confidence in God and afterwards undertakes the most difficult things, this action is not contrary to humility—above all when he considers that he rises so much the nearer to God in proportion as he submits to him the more profoundly by humility."[97]

And St. Augustine says, "It is one thing to raise oneself up to God, and another thing to raise oneself up against him. He who casts himself down before God is uplifted, and he who rises up against God is cast down by him."[98]

The chief fruit of humility is to make us so pleasing to God that his grace, meeting with no obstacles, abounds in us and brings us the assurance of remaining united to God by love: this is the state of perfect charity. After having explained the different degrees of humility, St. Benedict concludes his comments with a phrase that, although so short, is one of great depth and merits our special attention. "The monk who has ascended all these degrees of humility," he says, "will soon arrive at that perfect charity from which all fear is cast out."

You may have thought in the past that spiritual authors are at times at odds or uncertain when they have to regulate the rank of preeminence among the virtues. But it is beyond doubt that the queen of virtues is charity—and charity cannot exist in a soul without humility, which on account of our fallen nature is the condition sine qua non of the exercise of charity. Humility, then, is not perfection. Perfection, as we have said, consists in the love by which we remain, in all things, united through Christ to God and to God's will. But humility, also, as St. Thomas says, is "a disposition that facilitates the soul's free access to spiritual and divine goods."[99]

So charity is greater than humility, as the perfection of a state is greater than the dispositions requisite to reach that state. But humility, in achieving the work of removing the obstacles opposed to divine union, takes the first rank. Humility constitutes the very foundation of the spiritual edifice; it is the disposition that immediately precedes perfect charity. Without it and the work it does, the state of charity and of perfect union with God cannot exist, still less be maintained. Although humility is then in this sense a negative disposition, it is so necessary and so infallibly crowned by perfect charity that in a soul that does not possess it, the spiritual edifice is ever exposed to ruin for lack of foundation.

It is the sublime recompense of humility to contribute, more than any other virtue, in preparing the soul to the outpouring of the divine gifts that assure perfect union with God. "Nothing, in fact, is more sublime than this way of union," says St. Augustine, "but it is only the humble who walk in it."[100] It is not by exaltation, but by humility that we attain to God.

There is one more thing to say: that is, to explain the means of attaining this most indispensable virtue. The first of all means is prayer. A high degree of humility is a gift of God, as is a high degree of prayer. "Our Lord Himself," says St. Teresa, "supplies [acts of humility] in a way very different from that by which we could acquire them by our own poor reflections, which are as nothing in comparison with that real humility arising out of the light Our Lord here gives us."[101]

God—who infinitely desires to give himself to us—will never reject our prayer, if we beg him to take away the chief obstacle that's opposed to his action in our souls. We should beg God often for that spirit of reverence which is the very root of humility. Beg him to show you, in the light of his grace, that he is all and that without him we are nothing. One ray of divine light can do more in this way than any reasoning. Humility might be called the practical reflection of our intercourse with God.

A soul that does not frequently enter into contact with God in prayer cannot possess humility in a high degree. If even once God gave us to perceive, in the depth of our soul, in the light of his ineffable presence, some of his greatness, we would be filled with intense reverence for him. The groundwork of humility would be acquired and we would only have to guard faithfully this ray of divine light for humility to be developed and kept alive.

Let's give ourselves often to the consideration of divine perfections, not in a philosophic manner for the satisfying of the mind, but in a prayer and contemplation. "Believe me," says St. Teresa, "we will advance more [in humility] by contemplating the Divine than by keeping our eyes fixed on ourselves, poor creatures of earth that we are. . . . I believe we will never learn to know ourselves except by endeavoring to know God, for, beholding his greatness we are struck by our own baseness. His purity shows our foulness."[102] This is so true! The consideration of our own misery may produce a *passing* sense of humility, but the virtue, which is a habitual disposition, does not consist in this. Reverence toward God is the one way to give birth to the virtue, and render it stable.

If we frequently contemplate Christ Jesus in his passion, if we are united to him by faith, we may be assured that he will make us participate in his humility. We should never forget this profound truth: the sacred humanity of Jesus had its motive and power only in the Word to whom he was united. Christ's actions were truly his own because the human nature in Jesus was perfect, but their value was derived only from the union of the humanity with the divine Word.

It ought to be the same for us in the domain of our spiritual activity. We can do nothing of ourselves. We should humble ourselves in beholding the divine perfections and be penetrated with reverence. We should place all our confidence in our union with Jesus Christ through faith and love. In him, through him, with him, we are the children of the heavenly Father. That is the source of this confidence in which our lowliness finds its counterpart, and without which it would be an imperfect humility and an occasion of discouragement. To imagine that even with Christ's help we are incapable of good actions is to lose sight of the greatness of Jesus's merits; it is to lay open our soul to spiritual distrust and despair, which are the fruits of hell. By true humility we have no confidence in ourselves. Our power comes from God who naturally and supernaturally gives us being, life, and movement. And this power extends to all things, because we have boundless confidence in the merits of our divine head, Christ Jesus.

Chapter Seven

BONUM OBEDIENTIAE

THE FOUNDATION OF SPIRITUAL LIFE IS, AS WE HAVE seen, constituted in some way by humility, a virtue that is the preliminary and necessary disposition for the state "of perfect charity to be established in the soul."[103] But, as St. Benedict also shows, the practical expression of humility, with the monk, is obedience.

Indeed, when the soul is full of reverence toward God, it submits itself to God and to those who represent him in order to do his will in all things.[104] This is obedience. This virtue is the fruit and crown of humility.

Obedience, said God to St. Catherine of Siena in one of the dialogues, "has a nurse who feeds her; that is true humility. Therefore a soul is obedient in proportion to her humility, and humble in proportion to her obedience. . . . Without this nurse [which is humility], obedience would perish of hunger, for obedience soon dies in a soul deprived of humility."[105]

O bedience completes the work of abolishing any obstacles still opposed to divine union.

Poverty has removed the danger accruing from exterior belongings. The "conversion of manners" represses the tendencies of concupiscence and is careful to eliminate, in a general manner, all that, properly speaking, is imperfection.

Humility, going still further to the root of the matter, refrains all inordinate self-esteem. So, what still remains to be overcome? Self-will. That is the citadel of the ego. Once this will is surrendered, and it surrenders by obedience, all is given. The soul has nothing more belonging to it, nothing that it any longer possesses as its own. God can from this moment forward exercise his action over it in all plenitude: there are no more obstacles opposed to divine action.

By perfect obedience, men and women live in the truth of their being and of their condition: that is why this virtue is so fundamental and so pleasing to God. God, who has no need of anyone or anything, created us freely and by a movement of love. From this primordial fact, the essential relations between ourselves and God are derived. A creature is something essentially dependent upon God: "In him we live and move and have our being" (Acts 17:28).

Therefore it would be going against the eternal law not to recognize this condition by our entire dependence on God. What is the cry that should burst forth from the depths of our being as creatures? "Come, let us adore the Lord!" And why? For he is the Lord our God and he has made us. As reasonable creatures we ought to express our dependence by adoration and the submission of obedience.

We see God requiring this obedience throughout the history of the human race, at each page of the Bible. The great saints of the Old Testament shine in obedience; we hear them always renewing the cry repeated by Abraham, the father of believers: "Here I am!" Then, Christ's coming upon earth renders us the children of God and henceforward our obedience has taken a new shade of meaning, a new character: it is an obedience full of love. But this special seal placed upon our obedience, while giving it a special splendor, takes away nothing of its fundamental character that links it to humility and imbues it with reverence and faith.

I f obedience is infinitely pleasing to God, it is no less beneficial to
the soul. God reigns as master and sovereign in the obedient soul,
but as a sovereign who is infinitely good and lavishes his gifts and
graces upon it.

Obedience is named in the last place in the formula of our monastic
profession. In our vows it occupies supreme rank. Let us then study
its source—its nature—the qualities it ought to have—and from
what deviations it must be preserved.

For example, the principle that makes obedience so necessary
for us as monks is that this virtue resumes the means of finding
God. Why have we come to the monastery? What is our object
in living here? There is but one: to seek God, to tend toward him
with all the energies of our being. But it is by following Christ
Jesus that we find God, for it is he alone who brings humanity
back to God. So how does Christ achieve this gigantic work? By
his obedience. He declares that he has not come to do his own
will but that of his Father who sent Him (John 6:38). Obedience
is, as it were, his daily bread. We see him seeking above all things
to do always, under every circumstance, what pleases his Father.
As we've seen, he accepts the passion because it expresses his
Father's will (John 14:31).

Now, says the Apostle Paul, as it was through Adam's disobedience
that we became sinners and the enemies of God, so it was through
this obedience of Christ that we are justified and saved. A great
disobedience and a great obedience are the two factors of the loss
and salvation of the human race (Rom. 5:19). This obedience of

Christ is the means preordained by God for saving the world and restoring to it the heavenly inheritance. It was an expiation for the disobedience of Adam, our first father, and we go to God by uniting our obedience to that of Christ Jesus.

All the economy of God's designs for our sanctification converge for us in a state of obedience. When the Father sent his Son upon earth, what did he say to the Jews? "This is my Son, the Beloved. . . . [L]isten to him" (Matt. 17:5)! God might as well have said: Do what my Son asks you. Obey him. That is all I ask in order to give you my friendship.

Now that Christ has left us and ascended into heaven, he has given his powers to the Church: "All authority in heaven and on earth has been given to me. Go therefore and make disciples of all nations, baptizing them in the name of the Father and of the Son and of the Holy Spirit, and teaching them to obey everything that I have commanded you. And remember, I am with you always, to the end of the age" (Matt. 28:18–20).

The Church is invested with the authority of Jesus Christ. She speaks and commands in our Lord's name, and the essence of Catholicism consists in the submission of the intellect to Christ's teaching transmitted by the Church, and in the submission of the will to Christ's authority exercised by the Church.

Recall the scene in the Gospel described by St. John in his sixth chapter, Jesus speaks to the multitude of people whom he had miraculously fed on the previous day. He announces to them the Eucharistic bread: "I am the living bread that came down from heaven. Whoever eats of this bread will live forever" (John 6:51). At these words, his listeners are divided into two groups. The one begins to reason: "How can this man give us his flesh to eat?" How does Jesus act in the face of this reasoning? Does he give any explanation? No. He contents himself with affirming what he has just said with more insistency: "Very truly" (John 6:53). Then, no longer finding this "reasonable," they leave Christ. But there is another group formed of the apostles. In these same circumstances, what is their attitude? Do the disciples understand any better? No. But having faith in Christ's word, they remain with him to follow in his steps throughout all (see John 6:41–69).

Obedience of intellect and will is the way of life for every Christian, for every soul.

⟍⟋

Wat is true of the Christian is, a fortiori, true of the monk. Christ Jesus brings humanity back to his Father by his obedience, and every one must unite himself to Christ in obedience in order to find God. Not in this, or in anything else, does Christ separate himself from his mystical Body. A Christian must take his or her share in obedience and accept it in union with his Divine Head.

St. Benedict teaches no other doctrine than that of Christ and St. Paul. His words on this point are the direct echo of the Gospel and the teaching of the great apostle. At the very beginning of the Prologue he points out to us what is to be our end: "To return to God." Immediately afterward he indicates the means: we must return to God by obedience since it was by the sloth of disobedience that we turned away from him.

"To you therefore," he adds, "my words are now addressed that *renouncing your own will* in order to fight for the Lord Christ, our true King, is to *take in hand the strong and bright weapon of obedience.*" St. Benedict knows only one way of leading us to God, by union with Jesus Christ in his obedience: "Let the brothers know that it is by the path of obedience that they will come to God."[106]

The obedience of the Christian, while imposing certain sacrifices upon human nature, and certain duties to be fulfilled, leaves intact the free disposition that an individual has over his fortune, business, time, and activity. Simply put, Christian obedience is limited to the precepts contained in the Bible, and the commandments of the Church, which are themselves completed by each one's duties. God asks nothing more in order to give his heaven: "Why do you ask me about what is good? There is only one who is good. If you wish to enter into life, keep the commandments" (Matt. 19:17).

But there are souls whom love constrains to follow Christ more closely, that they may share his life of obedience more intimately. These souls hear the counsel of Jesus. For love of God, to give God greater glory, they seek a more exacting obedience than is imposed upon the simple faithful. An infallible supernatural intuition has revealed to them that it is more just, and they thereby give more adoration and more love to God.

By his profession, the monk strives to submit all that is in him to Christ. He does not wish anything to subsist that can be an obstacle to union between him and Christ. He wants to surrender to God his whole being and every detail of his life, because his adoration and his love aim at being perfect.

But as long as we hold the citadel of self-will we have not surrendered everything to God. We cannot say to our Lord in all truth: "Behold we have left all things and have followed you." When we give ourselves by obedience, we accomplish a supreme act of adoration and love toward God. Indeed there is one thing that is sacred to us even in God's sight. God touches our goods, the beings dear to us, our health, our existence. He is the absolute master of life and death; but there is one thing that he respects, namely, our liberty. He desires, with infinite desire, to communicate himself to us, and yet the action of his grace is, if I may thus express myself, subordinate to our acquiescence. That is, in a very real sense, our liberty is sovereign.

Now, in religious profession, we come before the altar and we take precisely what is most precious to us and out of love for God in order the better to confess his omnipotence. We immolate to him, in union with Christ, this "Isaac," this darling of our heart which is our liberty, and we give God full domain over our whole being and activity. Failing martyrdom, which is not at our disposal, we immolate ourselves as far as it depends upon us, by the vow of obedience. The sacrifice is immense; it is besides extremely pleasing to God.

"To leave the world and give up exterior possessions," says that great monk, St. Gregory, "is perhaps something easy, but for a man to give up himself, to immolate what is most precious to him by surrendering his entire liberty is a much more arduous work: to forsake what one *has* is a small thing; to forsake what one is, that is the supreme gift."[107] Without this gift, the sacrifice is not entire. "He is not detached from all," said St. Peter Damian, another holy monk, "who still retains himself; moreover, it serves for nothing to relinquish everything unless he relinquish himself."[108]

The gift we thus make of ourselves on the day of our profession subjects us to a definite obedience. We vow obedience "according to the Rule of St. Benedict." Consequently, we must understand the holy patriarch's concept of religious obedience. For there is obedience and then there is obedience, and as this virtue is one of the principles of our life, if the idea we form of it is erroneous, all our·monastic existence will be falsified.

There is an erroneous conception of obedience that no religious soul should accept. This conception makes of the superior a sage, an expert whom one has promised to consult, and to whom one goes out of prudence to learn what has to be done, and in order to avoid errors and mistakes. What the superior says is worth just what he knows, neither more nor less; his personal knowledge gives all the weight to his replies. This manner of seeing things misses the idea of submission, of homage paid to God in the person of another.

In religious obedience, there are different modes to be distinguished. Of course it is not here a question of criticizing anyone or anything whatsoever, because all the religious orders approved by the Church procure God's glory and are pleasing to him. My intention is only to lay stress, by way of comparison, on what is special in Benedictine obedience.

In some institutes, obedience is strongly marked with an economic character. Without ceasing to be the object of a vow and of a virtue, it is a means for arriving at a particular, special end, fixed by the constitutions of the order. Some orders or congregations have for their special end evangelization, another teaching, a third preaching. Obedience concurs in carrying out the particular work to which these institutes are dedicated. Those who belong to these orders and submit themselves generously to this obedience for love of our Lord surely attain holiness, because for them it is the vocation to which Christ has called them.

But with St. Benedict, obedience does not have this "economic" character. Obedience is to be desired in itself as the soul's homage to God, independently of the nature of the material work that is its object.

L et us suppose that the postulant in presenting himself at the monastery puts this question to the abbot: "What do you do here?" He will be told: "We go to God by following Christ in obedience." That is the sole end pursued. This is certainly the teaching of St. Benedict, for whom, to seek after God is the characteristic of the Benedictine vocation. And those who seek obedience may find God.[109]

In instituting monasticism, the great patriarch did not intend to create an order exclusively destined to attain such or such a particular end, or to accomplish such or such a special work. He wished only to make perfect Christians of his monks and envisaged for them the plenitude of Christianity. Doubtless, in the course of time, monasteries have become centers of civilization by preaching, the clearing and cultivation of land, teaching, art, and literary work, but this was only the outward blossoming, the natural and normal outcome of the fullness of Christianity with which these monasteries were inwardly animated. Being vowed to God, the monks spent themselves in the service of the Church, and under every form that this service demanded. But what they sought before all was to give to God, for love of him, the homage of all their being in obedience to an abbot, as Christ.

How is this will determined for the monk? By the Rule and the abbot. It is for the abbot, inspired by the Rule and respecting its traditions, to fix the direction of the activity of the monastery. Having, moreover, according to St. Benedict, to govern the monastery "wisely," he will undoubtedly be watchful to see how he may utilize, for God's glory and the benefit of the Church and society, the talents placed by God in each of his monks. But as for the monk himself, he has nothing to arrange or determine in all this: he does not come to the abbey to give himself to one occupation rather than another, to discharge such or such a function that he finds suitable. He comes to seek God in obedience. In this lies all his perfection.

You may perhaps say: This is inconceivable nonsense. Isn't it folly to submit oneself entirely in this way? Yes, from the merely human point of view it is, as monastic life taken as a whole is folly. But, replies St. Paul in his energetic language, "those who are unspiritual," that is, those who allow themselves to be guided by nothing but natural reason, "do not receive the gifts of God's Spirit, for they are foolishness to them" (1 Cor. 2:14). What is foolishness in the eyes of men is wisdom in the sight of God, and what is wisdom in the world's sight is foolishness before the Lord. And it has pleased God to confound the wisdom of the world with works of divine folly. For the wise of this world, wasn't it also folly and a scandal—the Greek philosophers of St. Paul's time certainly judged it so—for a God to have been made man in order to redeem humankind, and for thirty years to have lived a life of obedience in an obscure workshop, then consecrated three years to the labor of preaching before dying upon a cross? This was, however, the means chosen out of all others by God for the salvation of the human race. And this loving obedience, which was the mainspring of this life, had as its object an existence full of toil, of deep humiliation, and a death surrounded with indescribable sufferings. But it was by this that the world was redeemed. It is still thanks to this that the world continues to be saved, that souls return to God and are sanctified.

We can therefore understand why St. Benedict calls obedience "a good," *Bonum obedientiæ*.[110] What a remarkable expression! Does this mean we naturally like to obey? No, quite the contrary! Then why is obedience "a good," a thing that we ought to seek and hunger after?

Because it is the path by which a God has passed, a path that leads us to beatitude. Obedience gives us God. When we do God's will, we are united to God. And as we come to the monastery to seek God and obedience gives him to us, it becomes for us a precious good, for it gains us the sole Good.

Proportionately it is the same for us, since Christ is our model. True wisdom, that which is the gift of the Spirit, is to obey, to render to God the homage of our obedience, whatever be the material work that is the object of this obedience whereby it is manifested. For this reason St. Benedict says that true monks, those illumined with divine light, are only ambitious for eternal things, the things that alone are real.[111] They "desire"—and notice the word; St. Benedict does not say, "support"—obedience, as one seeks after a precious good that one may take possession of it.[112] They are on watch for occasions of obeying, and are thus enabled to give to God the most effectual pledge of their love.

This is the lofty concept that St. Benedict forms of obedience.

N ow, we have promised to follow his Rule so that we may live according to St. Benedict's spirit. It is this view of the matter that we must put into practice as far as we are able, because it is for us the path of perfection.

Obedience is then for the monk the surest way to holiness. St. Teresa calls it "the road that leads most rapidly to the summit of perfection" and "the promptest and also the most effectual means of arriving at perfection."[113] When a person achieves the work of giving himself entirely by obedience, he receives the Infinite Good in an incomparable measure.

You see how right our holy father St. Benedict is to insist so much upon this virtue? Let us try to understand thoroughly the character he wishes to give to it. Obedience is an homage of perfect submission of all our being to God. It is a good that we must unceasingly strive to obtain, for in it we shall find what we came to seek in the monastery, namely, God. If we never lose sight of this capital point, our obedience will become easy, whatever be the command given; and, through it, we shall obtain, with God, peace of soul and joy and freedom of heart.

L et us watch over ourselves. Obedience is too precious a good for us not to safeguard it with care. Let us love this good, this "bonum," as our holy father is pleased to call it, for it contains and gives God. Let us seek it with love and guard it jealously.

Let us think of the example given us by those who seek for gold. They are told that in some El Dorado, in some region unknown to them, gold is to be found. They set off with gladness, upheld by the hope of riches. They leave country, friends, and family. They embark, cross the seas, force their way through a thousand dangers, to the interior of unknown lands. Behold them at last, after many toils, perils, and explorations, arrived at the place where lies the precious metal. Now suppose that after having extracted it from the ground, at the cost of many pains and labors, they prepare to return without tak-ing back with them all that they can, but content themselves with a few nuggets held in their hands. What would we say of these men who have undergone so many sufferings, endured so many labors, overcome so many obstacles to content themselves finally with such meager gain? That they are fools. And we should be right.

Now, that is the portrait of a monk who, after some time spent in the monastery, suffers the loyalty of his obedience to be impaired. There is none among us that has not made great sacrifices before crossing the threshold of the cloister. We read one day in Holy Scripture, or we heard Christ give us in prayer, the counsel to leave all things and follow Him. This divine voice, full of sweetness, touched our soul to its depths. We understood the call of Jesus, and then, like the merchant in the Gospel, having found a treasure in a field, sold all that he had to gain this field and make himself master of the treasure. We left all things. We said farewell to all that was dear to us; we renounced the legitimate joys of hearth and home, the visible affection of our own dear ones. Why did we consent to all these acts of renunciation? To gain the treasure which is none other than God himself. And where do we find this treasure? In eternity we will find it in the ineffable and supreme bliss of God, here below in the obedience of faith. This is the treasure we seek and that obedience gives us. And after such great sacrifices, so often renewed, instead of appropriating this precious good in the greatest possible measure, will we content ourselves with taking some small pieces? Is it sufficient for us to obey from time to time, just enough not to fail in our vow? God grant it is not so, that we are not so foolish as thus to squander eternal treasures in advance!

Instead, let's live in obedience, making it "our food" as Christ himself did (John 4:34). Let's ask our Lord for this virtue of obedience in all its perfection, this virtue that surrenders the judgment, will, heart, the whole being to God and to his representative. If we are faithful in asking for this grace, Christ Jesus will certainly grant it to us. Each morning, let's join ourselves to Jesus in his obedience, in the entire submission that he made of himself at the moment of the Incarnation.

"This will may perhaps be painful to my nature, to my tastes; it may be opposed to my personal ideal, hard to my spirit of independence; but I want to offer you, Lord, this sacrifice as testimony of my faith in your word, of my confidence in your power, and of the love I bear to you and to your Son Jesus." We ought to renew this offering every day, even—and especially—if it happens that a work imposed or approved by our superior responds to our personal tastes. Otherwise, it is greatly to be feared that the natural satisfaction we may find in it will carry us away and make us forget that spirit of obedience with which our works ought to be done in order to be pleasing to God.[114]

If we act in this way, our obedience will be sanctified by contact with that of Jesus. He who infinitely desires that we be "one with Him" (John 17:21) will grant us to reach little by little the perfection not only of the vow, but of the virtue. And through this virtue, he will finish the work of detaching us from ourselves to unite us entirely to himself, since we shall no longer have any will but his own—and through him we will be united to the Father.

Chapter Eight

THE PEACE OF CHRIST

I N ALL THE PRECEDING CONFERENCES, I HAVE SOUGHT
to do only one thing: to place the divine figure of Christ Jesus
before your eyes, so that contemplating this unique ideal, you
may love and imitate it. This is in fact the whole of monasticism, and
the very substance of Christianity.

All these virtues, if carried to a certain degree of perfection, are
characteristic of the religious life and have their first exemplar in
Jesus: integral seeking after God, the entire gift of self, poverty,
humility, obedience, abandonment to the divine will, the spirit of
faith toward our heavenly Father, charity, and good zeal toward our
neighbor.

The one aim of monastic life is to make us perfect disciples of
Christ. We are truly monks only on condition that we are first of all
Christians. St. Benedict wrote his Rule only as an abridgment of the
gospel. This is why, in ending as in beginning the code destined for
his sons, he tells them nothing else than "to follow Christ."[115] "They
should prefer absolutely nothing before Christ who will bring us
to everlasting life."[116] It is with these words that the holy legislator
takes leave of us in the last chapter.

Now, when we desire to sum up the whole of Christ's work, to see in brief the extent of his mystery, what do we find to say? Is there one word in which can be gathered up the whole substance of the mystery of the Man-God? Yes, there is one word.

When Christ appeared upon earth, after thousands of years of waiting and anguish, what was the first message that fell from heaven, the message wherein human beings could discover in advance the secret of the ineffable mystery of the Word incarnate, and, as it were, the plan of all the work of Jesus? It was the message brought by the angels sent by God himself to announce to the world the good tidings of the birth of his Son: "Glory to God in the highest heaven, and on earth peace among those whom he favors" (Lk. 2:14)! The Word becomes incarnate to give all glory to his Father, and bring peace to the world. To seek his Father's glory is the supreme aspiration of Christ's heart. The gift of peace condenses in itself every good that the Savior brings to the souls he comes to redeem.

Christ's life on earth has but this one aim. When that is attained, he looks upon his work as finished. In the presence and hearing of his apostles, he says in that wonderful prayer to his Father: "I glorified you on earth by finishing the work that you gave me to do" (John 17:4). And at the same moment, what does he say to his disciples to show that, in regard to them, he has also "finished the work"? He leaves them peace, his own peace, not that which the world promises, but that which God alone can give (John 14:27). It is the perfect gift he leaves to his apostles, as to all souls redeemed and saved.

This gift of peace is so precious and so necessary for the preservation of every other gift that Jesus asks his disciples to greet one another with it (Lk. 10:5).

All the letters of St. Paul—the herald of the mystery of Christ—begin with a salutation such as this: "Grace to you and peace from God our Father, and from the Lord Jesus Christ." The apostle associates grace with peace, because grace is the primary condition of peace. "Without grace," says St. Thomas, "it is impossible to have true peace."[117]

This peace, like other every good gift, comes from God the Father as its first principle. This is why St. Paul throughout his epistles often designates the heavenly Father as "the God of peace."[118] This peace comes, too, from Christ: did he not gain it for us in giving, through his immolation, full satisfaction to divine justice? Then peace comes to us from the Holy Spirit: it is one of the fruits of the spirit of love, as much as is joy.

Peace is an essentially supernatural, an essentially Christian gift.

We cannot be astonished that St. Benedict places peace before us as a gift that we should eagerly seek after, and that the word *"pax"* has become one of our dearest mottos. It adorns the front of our monasteries. Inscribed on the threshold of our cloisters, it ought above all to be engraved in the depths of our hearts and emanate from our whole being. It is the word that best sums up, even in the eyes of seculars, the characteristic harmony of our life.

Peace, the supreme result of the practice of virtue in a heart given wholly to God, is the first good we wish to those who come to us. Faithful to the gospel precept and inheritor of the first ages of the Church, our holy father St. Benedict wills that the prior and brothers should give the kiss of peace to all guests who arrive at the monastery.[119]

But how can we truly wish this good to others if we do not possess it in ourselves? Let us then see what this peace is. What are its characteristics and what is the source from which it is to be derived?

⌣⟶

If we are to be worthy disciples of Christ and of St. Benedict we must seek this good—peace—as a great treasure. In the Prologue where he traces the broad outline of his institution, St. Benedict recalls the words of the psalmist: "Seek peace, and pursue it" (Ps. 34:14). It is remarkable that he associates the seeking after peace with the seeking after God, as two ends that become one. Indeed, theose who strive to find this peace for themselves and others are truly the children of God. He who is the infallible truth tells us so: "Blessed are the peacemakers, for they will be called children of God" (Matt. 5:9). Our holy father who wishes, throughout his Rule, to bring us to God and make us perfect children of the heavenly Father by the grace of Jesus, has ordained everything in the monastery in such a way "that all the members may be at peace."[120] With this conference on peace we will therefore finish determining the characteristics that mark the physiognomy of the monk, the disciple of Christ.

What then is peace? We are not talking about a question of exterior peace, that which results for us from solitude and silence. That is certainly a great thing, for silence and solitude help the faithful soul to be recollected, the better to turn to God. However, this outward peace is profitless if the imagination is wandering and the soul is troubled and disquieted. It is inward peace that I wish to speak to you about. You know the definition that St. Augustine has given of it: "Peace is the tranquillity of order."[121]

To understand the force of this sentence, let us carry our minds back to the days of the creation of Adam. It is said that God created humankind "straight," not "crooked," in perfect rectitude of nature

(Ecc. 7:13). He had given him sanctifying grace, original justice. All Adam's faculties were perfect and perfectly harmonized. In this virgin nature, from the hands of God, there was a magnificent subordination of the inferior powers to reason, of reason to faith, and of the whole being to God. There was a harmony that was the divine radiation of original justice. The order was perfect in Adam; complete concord reigned between all the faculties, each of which rested in its object. From all of this was born unalterable peace. As St. Thomas says, it is "from the union of the different appetites in man tending towards the same object that peace results."[122]

Sin came into the world and all this admirable order was overthrown. There was no longer union between man's different appetites. Diverse and contrary tendencies, generally in conflict, were henceforward to be encountered in him: the flesh conspires against the spirit, and the spirit wars against the flesh.

⟶

To find peace again, the desires must be brought back to order and unity. This order consists in the senses being dominated by reason and the reason being subject to God. Until such order is reestablished, peace cannot exist in the heart. "Thou hast made us for Thyself, O Lord, and our hearts are ever restless until they rest in Thee," says St. Augustine.[123]

But how are we to rest in God if sin has made us his enemies? In consequence of sin—Adam's sin and our own—far from being able to approach God, we are separated from him by an abyss. Is man then forever to be robbed of peace, is all his sighing after this lost possession to be in vain? No. Order is to be reestablished, and peace restored, and you know in what an admirable manner. It is in Christ and through Christ that both order and peace are to be found again, in his having restored to us God's friendship and given us his own infinite merits whereby we may retain this friendship.

St. Paul wrote to the Ephesians: "Now in Christ Jesus you who once were far off have been brought near by the blood of Christ. For he is our peace; in his flesh he has made both groups into one and has broken down the dividing wall, that is, the hostility between us" (Eph. 2:13–14). He says again: "Christ God was reconciling the world to himself, not counting their trespasses against them, and entrusting the message of reconciliation to us" (2 Cor. 5:19). Christ is the holy victim, perfectly pleasing to God and in him God has forgiven us.

Christ is the Prince of Peace. He has come to fight against the prince of darkness and snatch us from the power of the devil in order to make peace between God and man. This Prince of Peace is so magnificent in his victory that he gives us a share in all his merits in order that we may forever keep this peace won by his blood.

In the weeks following his resurrection, it is peace that Christ wishes to his apostles each time he appears to them. His passion expiated everything, paid off everything; therefore this salutation of peace, henceforward restored by his grace, falls continually from his divine lips.[124] Isn't it remarkable that this same wish of peace should be heard at the two extremities of his earthly career: when the angels announce the opening of his mission of salvation, and when, this being accomplished, he enters into his glorious life? "Peace be with you."

L ook at St. Paul. Tormented by the inward warfare of the flesh against the spirit, he cries out: "Who will rescue me from this body of death?" And what answer does he give to his own question? "Thanks be to God through Jesus Christ our Lord" (Rom. 7:24–25)! For, he adds, Christ by his death has freed us from all condemnation. His grace has been given to us so that we may live, not according to the desires of the flesh but according to those of the Spirit. And, he concludes, the desires and affections of the flesh bring forth death, the desires and affections of the Spirit bring life and peace (Rom. 8:1–6). It is then in the grace of Christ Jesus that the principle of peace is to be found. This is what makes us pleasing to God and gives us his friendship, making us see that other people are our brothers and sisters, subduing perverse tendencies in us, and making us live according to the divine will.

This grace comes to us only through Christ. For such is the divine order, the essential order: Christ Jesus has been established king over Zion. He is king by right of conquest, having delivered himself up to death for the souls he wills to bring back to his Father. He is this peaceful king who shows his magnificence in coming down from heaven to bring us pardon. The Father has given him all power in order that he may be our justice, sanctification, redemption, and "our peace" (Eph. 2:14).

Such is the admirable order established by God: Christ, the head of all the elect, is for each one of them the source of grace, the principle of peace. Outside this order there can only be trouble and insecurity for the soul. Those who want to do without God, those whom Scripture calls "the wicked" (Isa. 48:22) cannot have peace. Doubtless, certain of their desires can be satisfied, fulfilled even. They can satisfy to a certain point their thirst for pleasures and honors. But, this is an apparent and false peace, according to St. Thomas.[125] The impious are ignorant of what is truly good. They put the contentment of their desires in apparent, relative, fugitive goods. Thus, those souls who appear happy are never truly so; the heart remains empty even after having exhausted all the sources of joy that the creature can give, because our deepest desires exceed all sensible good.

All we can do on our own is in vain. Our hearts are created for God. This is one of the principles of order: our hearts have a capacity for the infinite and no creature can satisfy them perfectly. "Why," says St. Augustine, "do you persist in always traveling painful and wearisome paths? Rest is not where you are seeking it. . . . You pursue happiness in the journey of death; it is elsewhere. How will a happy life be found where there is not even true life?" Then he concludes: "He who is life, our life, has come down among us."[126]

In Christ Jesus alone is to be found the principle of life, the source of peace.[127] To enjoy true peace, we must then not only "seek God," but we must seek him in the way he wishes us to seek him, that is to say, in Christ. This is the fundamental order, established by God, according to the good pleasure of his sovereign will (see Eph. 1:9–10). Outside this order fixed by infinite wisdom, we can find neither holiness nor perfection; we can find neither peace nor joy.

In the center of the soul that loves God there rises up the "city of peace" that no noise of earth can trouble, that no attack can surprise. We may truly say that nothing that is exterior, outside us, can, unless we allow it, touch our inward peace. Our inward peace essentially depends on only one thing: our attitude toward God. It is in him that we must trust. "The LORD is my light and my salvation; whom shall I fear?" (Ps. 27:1). If the wind of temptation and trial arises, I only have to take refuge with him. "Lord, save us! We are perishing!" Our Lord, when the ship was tossed about by the waves, calmed the tempest with a single gesture. So too now there will come a great calm (Matt. 8:25–26).

If we really seek God in everything, by following in the footsteps of Christ, who is the sole way that leads to the Father, if we strive to be detached from all, that we may only desire the master's good pleasure, if, when the Spirit of Jesus speaks to us, there is no inflexibility of soul and us and no resistance to his inspirations, we may be assured that peace, deep and abundant, will reign in us. For Lord, "Great peace have those who love your law" (Ps. 119:165). Souls that do not wish to give all to Our Lord, to bring all their desires to unity by this total donation, cannot taste this true peace. They are divided, tossed to and fro between themselves and God, between the satisfaction of their self-love and obedience. They are the prey of trouble and disquiet.

Even its past sins do not trouble the soul established in peace. Certainly it feels profound sorrow in having offended the heavenly Father, in having caused the sufferings of Jesus and grieved the Spirit, but this sorrow is not mixed with agitation and fever. The soul knows that Jesus is the ransom for sin, and a ransom of infinite value, that he has become "the atoning sacrifice for our sins, and not for ours only but also for the sins of the whole world" (1 John 2:2).

The soul knows that Christ is at the right hand of the Father, ever living, a compassionate high priest who unceasingly pleads in our favor (Heb. 7:25). Nothing gives such peace to a contrite soul as to be able to offer to the Father all the sufferings, expiations, satisfactions, and merits of his beloved Son. Nothing gives the soul such confidence as to be able to render to him, through Jesus, all glory and praise. For this homage of Christ, which the soul makes its own, is full, adequate, leaving nothing to be desired. It gives deep peace to the soul that finds in Jesus the perfect means of repairing all its negligences and all its faults.

Discouragement also cannot penetrate into this soul to trouble it; it knows something of "the boundless riches of Christ" (Eph. 3:8). Certainly, by itself it can do nothing, not even have a good thought, but it submits to the order willed by God, the author of the supernatural life and it knows that in this order is likewise contained the power the soul has of appropriating to itself the riches of Jesus. "I can do all things through him who strengthens me" (Phil. 4:13). Its confidence cannot be shaken, because the soul belongs to him who is for it The Way.

Finally, death cannot trouble the soul that has only sought God. It has confided itself to the One who says: "Those who believe in me, even though they die, will live" (John 11:25). Our Lord is the truth; he is also the life; and he brings us, restores to us, the life that is unending. Even though the shadow of death falls upon it, the soul that has sought only God will abide in peace. It know the presence of Christ Jesus. This presence reassures us against every terror.

In one of her "Exercises," St. Gertrude allows her assurance, which the infinite merits of Jesus give her, to overflow. At the thought of the divine tribunal, an image that rises up before her mind, she makes the most moving appeal to these merits. "Woe unto me, if, when I come before you, I had no advocate to plead my cause! O Love, stand forth on my behalf, answer for me, sue out my pardon. If you undertake my cause, I know that I still have hope of life. I know what I will do, I will take the chalice of salvation, even the chalice of my Jesus. I will lay it upon the empty scale of the balance of Truth. So shall I supply all that is lacking, and outweigh all my sins. . . . Come with me to judgment," says St. Gertrude to our Lord.[128]

For souls moved by such sentiments, death is only a transition. Christ comes to open to them the gates of the heavenly Jerusalem, which much more than ever in the past deserves to be called the a blessed vision of peace. There will be no more darkness, trouble, tears, or sighs, only peace—infinite and perfect peace. "Peace first becomes ours with the longing and seeking for the Creator. Then, it is in the full vision and eternal possession of him that peace is made perfect," writes St. Gregory.[129]

L et us then ask Jesus to bring us to this peace that is the fruit of his love. "Lord God, give peace to us," as St. Augustine says at the end of his *Confessions*, that wonderful book where he shows us how he sought peace in every possible satisfaction of the senses, the mind, and the heart, everywhere but in God, to no avail. "Give peace to us . . . the peace of the Sabbath, a peace without any night." And the holy Doctor who had made the experience of all things, who had felt the vanity of every creature, the frailty of all human happiness, ends the book with this cry: "So shall it be received, so shall it be found, so shall it be opened."[130]

On the day of our professions we relinquished everything, we gave ourselves to Jesus so that we might follow him. We only have to continue in this disposition and we will taste peace. Everything in the holy Rule is ordered in such a way as to procure this peace. Everything leads us to it. And the monastery, where men live according to this Rule, is indeed, even here below, a "vision of peace." Each one who lets himself be fashioned and molded by humility, obedience, the spirit of abandonment, and confidence— the foundations of the monastic life—becomes a city of peace.

Our souls are made for God and unless they are set toward this end, they are perpetually in agitation and trouble. St. Benedict wishes that we should have but this one and universal intention: that we should seek God.[131] He makes everything converge to this: this is the center of his Rule. By the unity of this end, he brings unity into all the manifold actions of our life, and especially into the desires of our being. This is, according to St. Thomas, one of the essential elements of peace.[132] Our souls are troubled when they are torn by desires that bear upon a thousand different objects,[133] but when we seek God alone by an obedience full of abandonment and love, we sum up all things in the one thing necessary. This establishes strength and peace within us.

Such is, in brief, the whole of the divine order—shown by our holy legislator St. Benedict with an admirable simplicity of approach. To return to God by Christ, to seek God in Christ, to tend toward God in the footsteps of Christ. And so as to prove that this seeking after God is sincere, absolute, and total: separation from the world, humility, loving obedience, the spirit of abandonment and confidence, the preponderance given to the life of prayer, the love of our neighbor. These are virtues of which Christ has given us the first example. Their exercise proves that we truly seek God, that we prefer absolutely nothing to the love of Jesus, that we make him our one and only ideal.

Happy is the monk who walks in this path! Even in the greatest sufferings, in the most painful temptations, in the most trying adversities, he will find light, peace, and joy. Everything is ordered in his soul as God wills it and all his desires are unified in the one sole good for whom he is created.

Speaking from experience, St. Benedict could guarantee for us the obtaining of many and great things. In as far, he says, that a monk goes forward in the way of faith and the practice of the virtues, it is "with heart enlarged that he runs with unutterable sweetness of love in the way of God's commandments."[134] Happy, once again, is this monk! Divine peace dwells in his soul, it is reflected upon his countenance, it is shed around him. He is essentially what St. Benedict wishes the monk to be: the child of God through Christ's grace, a perfect Christian.[135] Blessed, indeed, because God is with him, and at every moment he finds in this God, whom he came to the monastery to seek, the greatest and most precious good, because he is the supreme and unchanging good who never disappoints the desire of those who seek him in the simplicity and sincerity of their hearts.

NOTES

1 Holy Rule, ch. I.

2 S. Thomas, II *Sentent. Dist.* XXXVII, q. I a. 2.

3 Cf. *Of the Ecclesiastical Hierarchy.*

4 Ibid., chap. LVII.

5 St. Ambrose.

6 Cf. Psalm 33:9.

7 *Life of Raymund of Capua.*

8 *Life of St. Teresa by Herself,* ch. 11. Translated from the Spanish by David Lewis.

9 D. du Bourg, *La Bse J. M. Bonomo, moniale bénédictine,* Paris, 1910, p. 56.

10 Office of St. Agnes, 1st Ant. I Noct.

11 S. Augustine, *Confessions.* Lib. I, c.i.

12 Prologue to the Rule.

13 L. c. p. 145.

14 Prologue to the Rule.

15 S. Augustine, *De Trinitate,* I, XV, c. 28.

16 S. Gregory, *Dialog,* Lib. II, C, VIII.

17 Blosius, *The Mirror of the Soul,* ch. X, 7.

18 Rule, ch. 4.

19 Ibid., ch. 5.

20 Ibid., ch. 72.

21 Ibid., ch. 4; cf. Matthew 16:24.

22 Rule, ch. 5.

23 Ibid., ch. 4.

24 Prologue to the Rule.

25 Ibid.

26 Rule, chs. 2 and 63.

27 Ibid., ch. 2.

28 Ibid., ch. 36.

29 Ibid., ch. 53.

30 Ibid.

31 Ibid.

32 Ibid., ch. 4.

33 Ibid., chs. 4, 5, and 72.

34 Card. Gasquet, *Religio Religiosi: The Object and Scope of the Religious Life.*

35 I-II, q. LXXXVII, a. 4 and II-II, q. CLXII, a. 6.

36 Rule, ch. 58.

37 Ibid., ch. 4.

38 Ibid.

39 Ibid., ch. 7.

40 Epist. CXXX, ch. X.

41 Rule, ch. 52.

42 Ibid., ch. 20.

43 Ibid., ch. 7.

44 *Epistolæ*, Lib. VII, cf. 25.

45 *The Herald of Divine Love*, Book I, ch. XII.

46 *The Interior Castle*, translated by the Benedictines of Stanbrook, p. 202.

47 *Treatise on the Love of God*, Book XI, ch. XXI.2. Translated by the Rev. H. B. Mackey, OSB.

48 Sermon XLVII of the appendix to the works of St. Augustine. P.L. 39, col. 1838.

49 *Homil. In Evangel.*, lib. II, hom XXXI, 8. P.L. 76, col. 1232.

50 Rule, ch. 4.

51 Ordinary of the Mass, prayer before Communion.

52 Bossuet, *Meditations upon the Gospel*, Sermon on the Mount, 4th day.

53 S. Augustine, *Enarrat. In Ps.* 86:5.

54 Collect for the Saturday after Ash Wednesday.

55 Collect for Ash Wednesday.

56 Rule, ch. 49.

57 *Sermo X de Verbis Domini.* P.L. 38, Sermon 69.

58 Matthew 20:20–28.

59 Rule, ch. 72.

60 Ibid., ch. 13.

61 Ibid., ch. 4.

62 Ibid., ch. 13.

63 S. Aug. *L.c.*

64 Prologue of the Rule.

65 Rule, ch. 53.

66 Ibid. ch. 7.

67 Romans 8:37 and Rule, ch. 7.

68 1 Corinthians 9:7 and Rule, ch. 5.

69 Rule, ch. 4.

70 This is the teaching that God gave to St. Catherine. See *Dialogue on the Gift of Discernment*, ch. 7.

71 1 Corinthians 7:7 and Rule, ch. 40.

72 *Dialogue*, ch. 10.

73 Romans 6:6. Cf. D. Morin, *The Ideal of the Monastic Life in the Apostolic Age*, ch. 3. *Do penance*. This perfectly characterizes St. Benedict's method on this point.

74 Luke 24:26.

75 *Life of St. Teresa by Herself*, ch. 11.

76 Rule, ch. 33.

77 Ibid., ch. 32.

78 Ibid., ch. 31.

79 Ibid., ch. 58.

80 *Dialog.*, L. II, c. xxxv.

81 Cf. Colossians 2:3.

82 *De consideration*, Lib. V, cap. XIV, 32.

83 *Tractatus de moribus et officio episcope*, cap. V, 17.

84 *In Annuntiat.* B.M.V. Sermo III, 9, cf. *Epistola* CCCXCIII, 2–3.

85 *Sermo* 10 *de verbis Domini*.

86 *Humilitas…præbet hominem subditum et patulum ad suscipiendum influxum divinæ gratiæ, Cf.* S. Thomas, II-II, q. CLXI, a. 5, ad 2.

87 Cf. S. Thomas, II-II, q. CLXI, a. 4.

88 Rule, ch. 7. This idea seems to have been borrowed from St. Jerome: but this holy Doctor understands it of interior ascension by the exercise of all the virtues: *Scalam…per quam diversis virtutum gradibus ad superna conscenditur* (Epist., 983); St. Benedict restricts the idea to the practice of humility. Let us add then that in the sixth century, St. John Climacus wrote his celebrated *Scala paradise*, the "ladder that leads to Heaven," and that comprises thirty degrees, to recall the thirty years of Christ's hidden life.

89 *Summa theologica*, II-II, q. CLXI, a. 6, and q. CLXII, a. 4, ad 4.

90 Rule, ch. 4.

91 II-II, q. CLXI, a. 2, ad 3. Cf. a. I, ad 5; *Humilitas præcipue respicit subjectionem hominis ad deum.—Humilitas proprie respicit reverentiam qua homo deo subjicitur.*

92 II-II, q. CLXI, a. 4, ad 1.

93 Rule, ch. 7. The texts of the Rule cited in this Conference in regard to humility being all from Chapter VII, we refer the reader to it once for all.

94 Psalm 34:11.

95 *Life of St. Teresa by Herself*, ch. 10. Cf. also St. Francis of Sales, *Introduction to the Devout Life*, 3rd part, ch. 5.

96 Rule, ch. 4.

97 II-II, q. LCXI, a. 2, ad 2.

98 *Aliud est se levare ad Deum, aliud est levare se contra Deum. Qui ante illum se projicit ab illo erigitur; qui adversus illum se erigit ab illo projicitur.* Sermo 351. *De utilitate poenitentiæ.*

99 II-II, q. CLXI, a. 5, ad 4.

100 *Enarrat. in Psalm.* CXLI, c. 7.

101 *Life of St. Teresa by Herself*, ch. 15.

102 *The Interior Castle*, first Mansions, ch. 2, p.10

103 Rule, ch. 71.

104 II-II, q. CLXI, a. 3; a. I, ad 5.

105 *Dialogue*, translated by Algar Thorold, pp. 283–84, 302. The *Dialogue* contains an excellent treatise on *Obedience*. The Saint relates, in magnificent terms, the praise of obedience as she heard it from the Eternal Father.

106 Rule, ch. 71.

107 *Et fortasse laboriosum non est homini relinquere sua, sel valde laboriosum est relinquere semetipsum. Minus quippe est abnegare quod habet; valde autem multum est abnegare quod est. Homil.* 32 *in Evang.* P.L. 76, 1233. Cf. St Mechtilde, The Book of Special Grace, 4th part, ch. 17. *How our Lord clasps in His arms those who vow obedience.*

108 S. Petr. Damian, *In natale S. Benedicti*, P.L. 144, 549.

109 Prologue of the Rule.

110 Ibid., ch. 71.

111   Ibid., ch. 5.

112   Ibid.

113   *Foundations*, ch. 5.

114   This is the counsel that St. Gregory gives us: *Obedientiæ sibi virtutem evacuate qui ad prospera etiam et proprio desiderio anhelat. Moralia*, lib. XXXV. C. 14. P.L. 76, 706.

115   Prologue of the Rule.

116   Rule, ch. 72.

117   II-II, q. XXIX, a. 3, ad I.

118   Psalm 15:53; 16:20; 1 Corinthians 14:33, etc.

119   Rule, ch. 53.

120   Ibid., ch. 34.

121   *De civitate Dei*, L. XIX, ch. 13, P.L. 41, col. 640.

122   II-II, q. XXXIX, a. I.

123   *Confess*. Lib. I, c. I. P.L. 32, col. 661.

124   Luke 24:37; John 20:19, 26.

125   II-II, q. XXIX, a. 2, ad 3.

126   *Confess*. Lib. IV, c. 12. P.L. 32, col. 701.

127   Rule, ch. 58.

128   *Exercises of St. Gertrude*. Seventh Exercise: Reparation: Translated by Thomas Alder Pope, M.A., of the Oratory.

129   S. Gregory. *Moralia in Job*, Lib. VI, c. XXXIV, P.L. 75, col. 758.

130   *Confess*. Lib. XIII, c. 35 and 38.

131   Rule, ch. 58.

132   II-II, q. XXIX, a. 1, ad 1; a. 3.

133   Luke 10:41.

134   Prologue of the Rule.

135   Matthew 5:9.

ABOUT PARACLETE PRESS

WHO WE ARE

Paraclete Press is a publisher of books, recordings, and DVDs on Christian spirituality. Our publishing represents a full expression of Christian belief and practice—from Catholic to Evangelical, from Protestant to Orthodox.

We are the publishing arm of the Community of Jesus, an ecumenical monastic community in the Benedictine tradition. As such, we are uniquely positioned in the marketplace without connection to a large corporation and with informal relationships to many branches and denominations of faith.

WHAT WE ARE DOING

Paraclete Press Books

Paraclete publishes books that show the richness and depth of what it means to be Christian. Although Benedictine spirituality is at the heart of all that we do, we publish books that reflect the Christian experience across many cultures, time periods, and houses of worship. We publish books that nourish the vibrant life of the church and its people—books about spiritual practice, formation, history, ideas, and customs.

We have several different series, including the best-selling Paraclete Essentials and Paraclete Giants series of classic texts in contemporary English; Voices from the Monastery—men and women monastics writing about living a spiritual life today; award-winning poetry; best-selling gift books for children on the occasions of baptism and first communion; and the Active Prayer Series that brings creativity and liveliness to any life of prayer.

Mount Tabor Books

Paraclete's Mount Tabor Books series focuses on liturgical worship, art and art history, ecumenism, and the first millennium church.

Paraclete Recordings

From Gregorian chant to contemporary American choral works, our music recordings celebrate sacred choral music through the centuries. Paraclete Recordings is the record label of the internationally acclaimed choir Gloriæ Dei Cantores, praised for their "rapt and fathomless spiritual intensity" by *American Record Guide*, and the Gloriæ Dei Cantores Schola, which specializes in the study and performance of Gregorian chant. Paraclete Press is also the exclusive North American distributor of the recordings of the Monastic Choir of St. Peter's Abbey in Solesmes, France, long considered to be a leading authority on Gregorian chant.

Paraclete Video Productions

Our DVDs offer spiritual help, healing, and biblical guidance for life issues: grief and loss, marriage, forgiveness, anger management, facing death, and spiritual formation.

Learn more about us at our website
www.paracletepress.com or
phone us toll-free at 1.800.451.5006

SCAN
TO
READ
MORE

You may also enjoy these products from Paraclete Press . . .

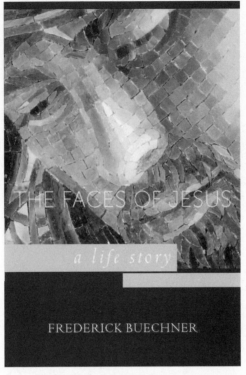

THE FACES OF JESUS
A Life Story

Frederick Buechner

ISBN: 978-1-61261-590-5 | $14.99 | Paperback

With timeless insight, award-winning author Frederick
Buechner introduces readers to the Jesus of the Gospels.
The old, old story rings new as Buechner revisits the ancient
stories, giving a distinctive and affectionate look at this person,
this God, this teacher, this wanderer, this man of suffering.

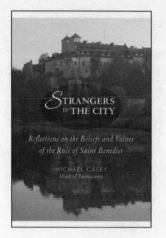

STRANGERS TO THE CITY

Reflections on the Beliefs and Values of the Rule of Saint Benedict

Michael Casey, ocso

ISBN: 978-1-61261-397-0 | $15.99 | Paperback

One of the world's most eloquent and incisive experts on monastic spirituality presents thoughtful reflections on the beliefs and values of asceticism, silence, leisure, reading, chastity, and poverty—putting these traditional Benedictine values into the context of modern life and the spiritual aspirations of people today.

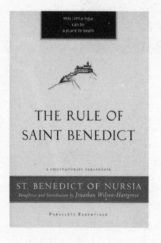

THE RULE OF SAINT BENEDICT

St. Benedict of Nursia
Paraphrase and Introduction by Jonathan Wilson-Hartgrove

ISBN: 978-1-55725-973-8 | $13.99 | Paperback

Jonathan Wilson-Hartgrove's vital, new, contemporary paraphrase includes the entire text of the Rule, plus a lengthy introduction from Jonathan and detailed explanatory notes throughout that explain difficult passages. The result is a classic reintroduced that will enliven any twenty-first-century expression of religious community.